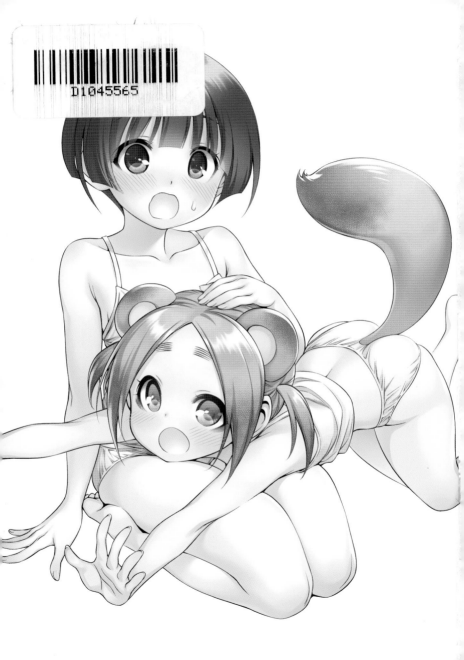

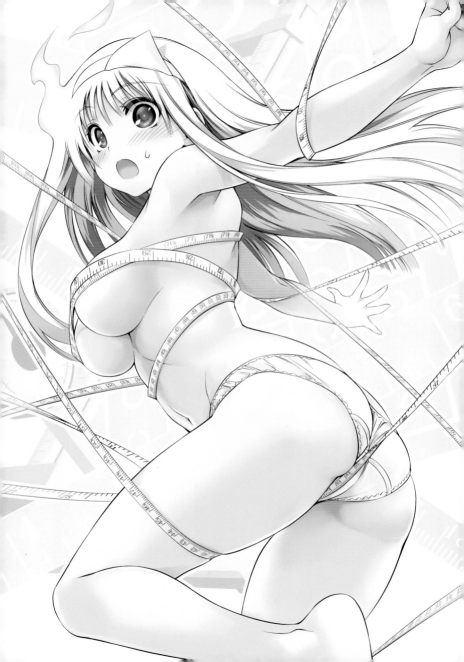

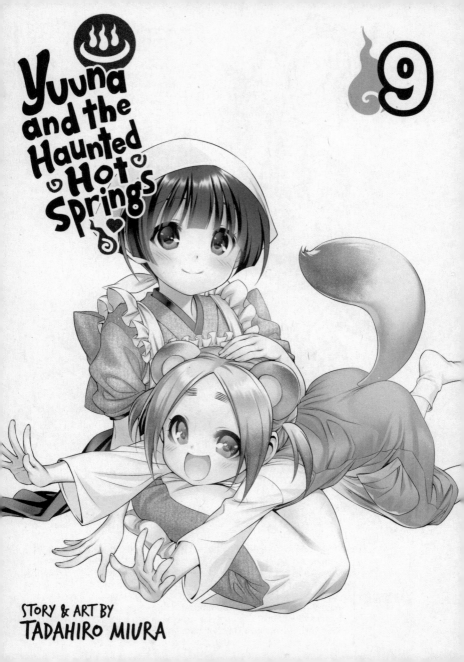

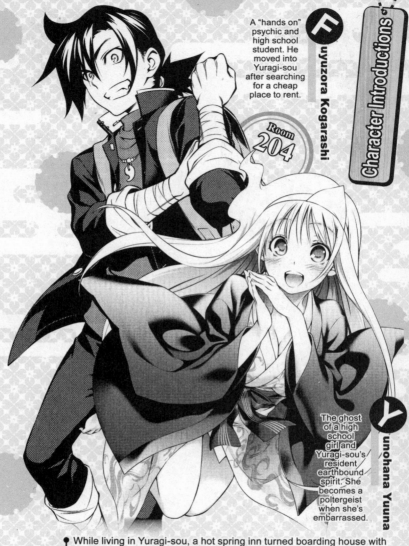

A "hands on" psychic and high school student. He moved into Yuragi-sou after searching for a cheap place to rent.

Fuyuzora Kogarashi

Room 204

The ghost of a high school girl and Yuragi-sou's resident earthbound spirit. She becomes a poltergeist when she's embarrassed.

Yunohana Yuuna

Summary

While living in Yuragi-sou, a hot spring inn turned boarding house with an unusual history, "hands on" psychic Fuyuzora Kogarashi promised Yuuna, the earthbound spirit of a high school girl, that he would make her happy and help her pass on. However, the daughter of Kyoto's Daitengu, Hiougi Karura, cast a spell on Kogarashi and attempted to force him into a shotgun wedding. Fortunately for Kogarashi, Yuuna used her poltergeist powers to break through her restraints and halted the ceremony. Meanwhile, Valentine's Day had come to Yuragi-sou and Kogarashi, the lucky dog, received many chocolates...♥

Room 202

A member of the Demon Slayer Ninja Force, a group of psychic ninjas who fight yokai. She's actually very shy.

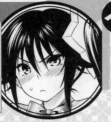

A meno Sagiri

Room 201

A sexy young lady who drinks *waaay* too much. She's an oni and the descendant of the big bad Shuten-douji.

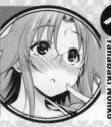

A rahabaki Nonko

Room 205

A holy sword who serves the House of Ryuuga. She intends to have Kogarashi's child in order to make the Ryuuga clan stronger.

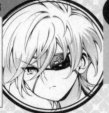

S hintou Oboro

Room 203

A sleepy-looking catgirl adored by nekogami. She has cat ears and a tail.

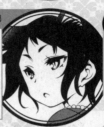

F ushiguro Yaya

Caretaker's Room

Despite her youthful appearance, she's a zashiki-warashi and Yuragi-sou's oldest resident. She can manipulate people's luck.

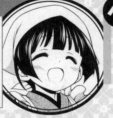

N akai Chitose

Room 206

Sagiri's cousin and member of the Demon Slayer Ninja Force. She is innocent and shy about her small chest size.

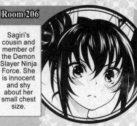

A meno Hibari

The most beautiful and popular girl in Kogarashi's class. She has a naughty imagination.

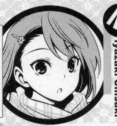

M iyazaki Chisaki

Caretaker's Room

A young bake-danuki girl. She looks up to Chisaki and is studying her boobs.

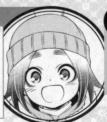

S higaraki Koyuzu

An extremely powerful yokai known as a Nue. Her hobby is picking fights and she's always in search of stronger opponents.

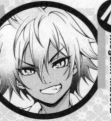

M ikogami Matora

The daughter of the daitengu who governs over the yokai of Kyoto. She's a genius who researches various techniques and resurrects them in the present day.

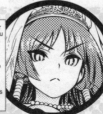

H iougi Karura

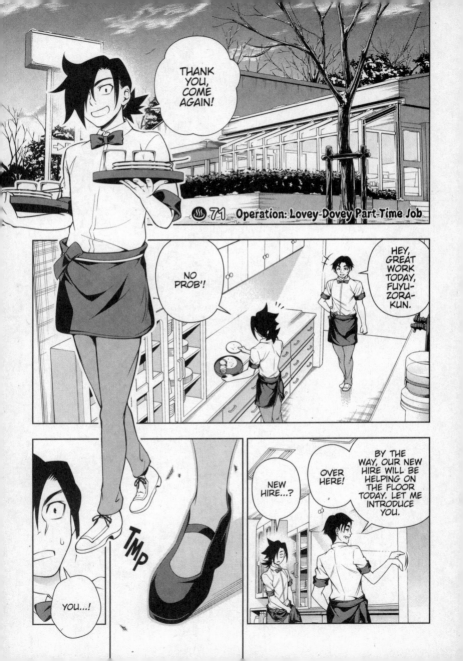

THANK YOU, COME AGAIN!

71 Operation: Lovey-Dovey Part-Time Job

NO PROB'!

HEY, GREAT WORK TODAY, FUYUZORA-KUN.

TMP

YOU...!

NEW HIRE...?

OVER HERE!

BY THE WAY, OUR NEW HIRE WILL BE HELPING ON THE FLOOR TODAY. LET ME INTRODUCE YOU.

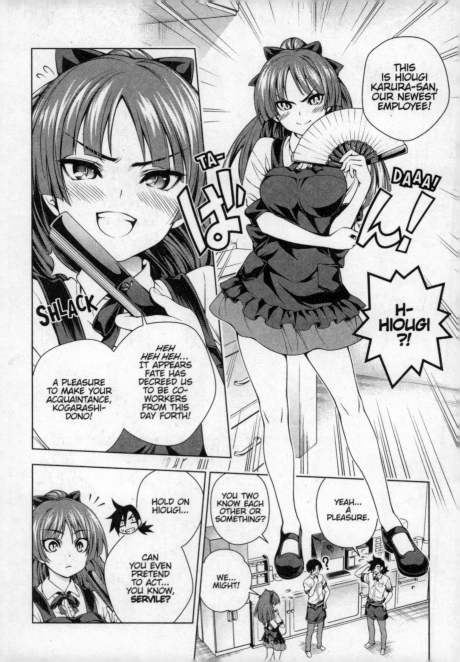

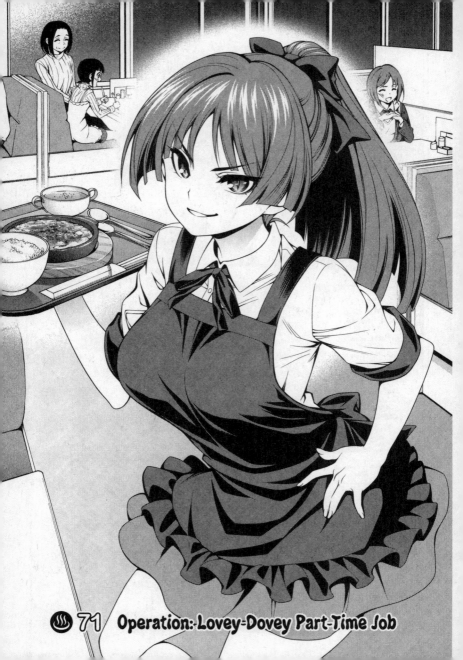

71 Operation: Lovey-Dovey Part-Time Job

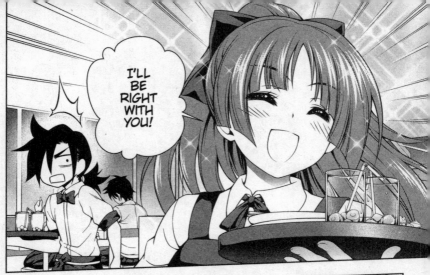

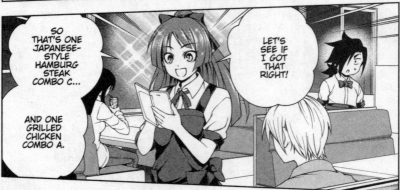

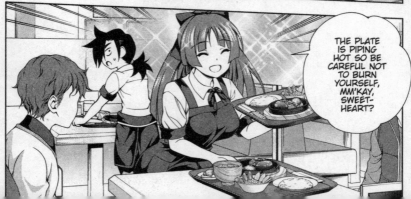

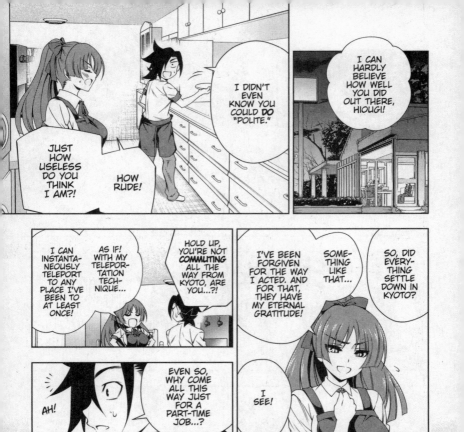

JUST HOW USELESS DO YOU THINK I AM?!

HOW RUDE!

I DIDN'T EVEN KNOW YOU COULD **DO** "POLITE."

I CAN HARDLY BELIEVE HOW WELL YOU DID OUT THERE, HIOUGI!

I CAN INSTANTANEOUSLY TELEPORT TO ANY PLACE I'VE BEEN TO AT LEAST ONCE!

AS IF! WITH MY TELEPORTATION TECHNIQUE...

HOLD UP, YOU'RE NOT **COMMUTING** ALL THE WAY FROM KYOTO, ARE YOU...?!

I'VE BEEN FORGIVEN FOR THE WAY I ACTED. AND FOR THAT, THEY HAVE MY ETERNAL GRATITUDE!

SOMETHING LIKE THAT...

SO, DID EVERYTHING SETTLE DOWN IN KYOTO?

AH!

EVEN SO, WHY COME ALL THIS WAY JUST FOR A PART-TIME JOB...?

I SEE!

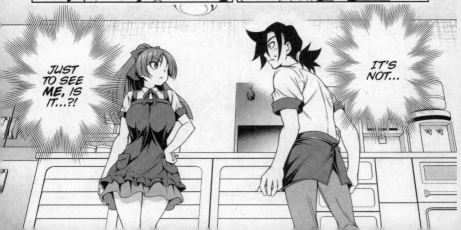

JUST TO SEE ME, IS IT...?!

IT'S NOT...

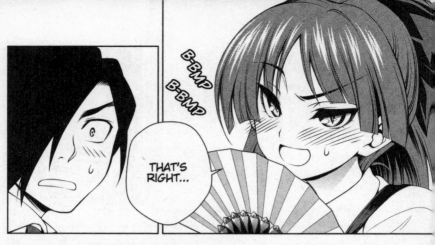

B-BMP
B-BMP

THAT'S RIGHT...

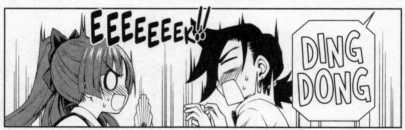

EEEEEEEK!!

DING DONG

NOT BAD...!

THAT WENT WELL, IF I SAY SO MY-SELF!!

CLAK

I'LL... I'LL TAKE CARE OF IT!

G... GUESS THAT'S OUR CUE.

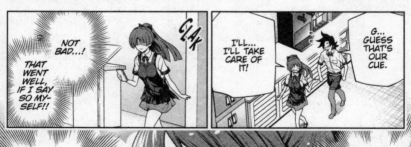

IS OFF TO A VERY PROMISING START!!

"OPERATION: LOVEY-DOVEY PART-TIME JOB TOGETHER..."

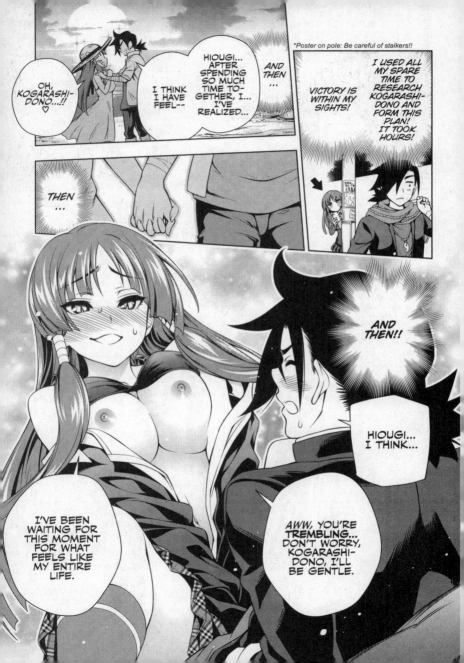

*Poster on pole: Be careful of stalkers!!

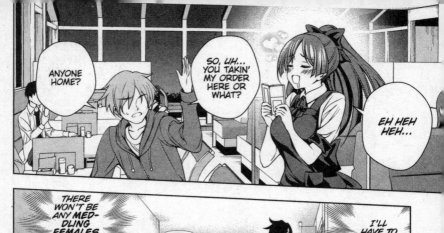

ANYONE HOME?

SO, UH... YOU TAKIN' MY ORDER HERE OR WHAT?

EH HEH HEH...

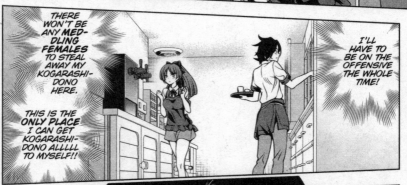

THERE WON'T BE ANY MEDDLING FEMALES TO STEAL AWAY MY KOGARASHI-DONO HERE.

THIS IS THE ONLY PLACE I CAN GET KOGARASHI-DONO ALLLLL TO MYSELF!!

I'LL HAVE TO BE ON THE OFFENSIVE THE WHOLE TIME!

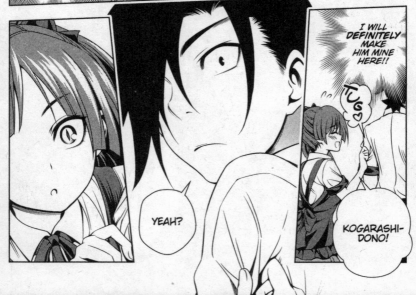

I WILL DEFINITELY MAKE HIM MINE HERE!!

YEAH?

KOGARASHI-DONO!

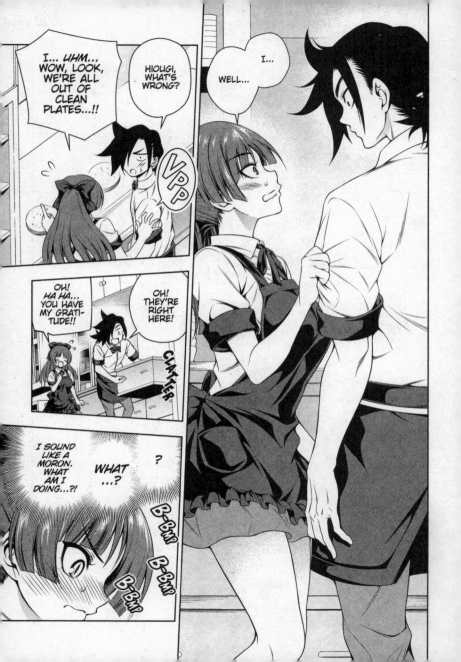

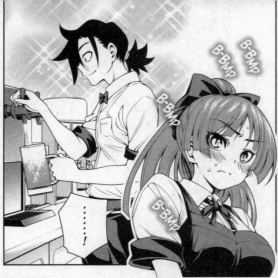

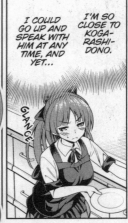

I'M SO CLOSE TO KOGA-RASHI-DONO.

I COULD GO UP AND SPEAK WITH HIM AT ANY TIME, AND YET...

GLANCE

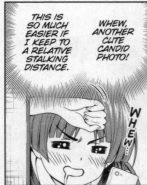

THIS IS SO MUCH EASIER IF I KEEP TO A RELATIVE STALKING DISTANCE.

WHEW, ANOTHER CUTE CANDID PHOTO!

WHEW...

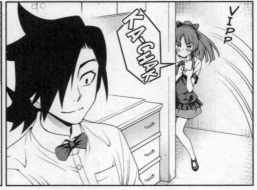

KA-CHAK!

VIPP

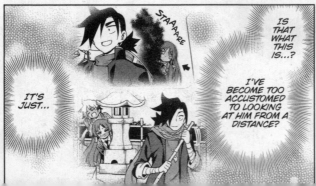

STAAAARE

IT'S JUST...

IS THAT WHAT THIS IS...?

I'VE BECOME TOO ACCUSTOMED TO LOOKING AT HIM FROM A DISTANCE?

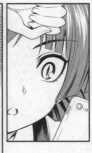

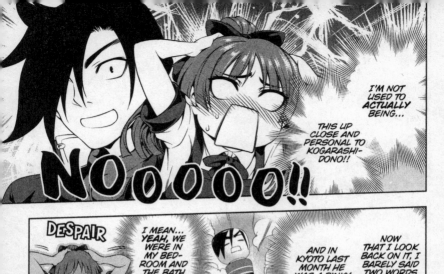

I'M NOT USED TO ACTUALLY BEING...

THIS UP CLOSE AND PERSONAL TO KOGARASHI-DONO!!

NOooooo!!

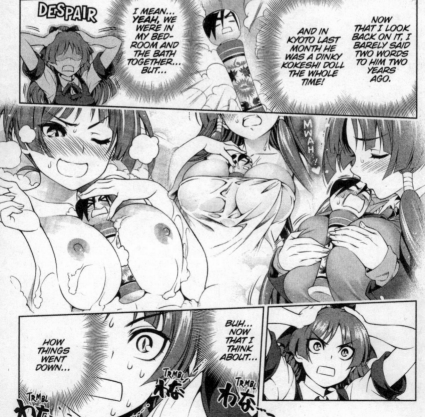

DESPAIR

I MEAN... YEAH, WE WERE IN MY BED-ROOM AND THE BATH TOGETHER... BUT...

AND IN KYOTO LAST MONTH HE WAS A DINKY KOKESHI DOLL THE WHOLE TIME!

NOW THAT I LOOK BACK ON IT, I BARELY SAID TWO WORDS TO HIM TWO YEARS AGO.

MWAH!!

HOW THINGS WENT DOWN...

BUH... NOW THAT I THINK ABOUT...

TRMBL

TRMBL

TRMBL

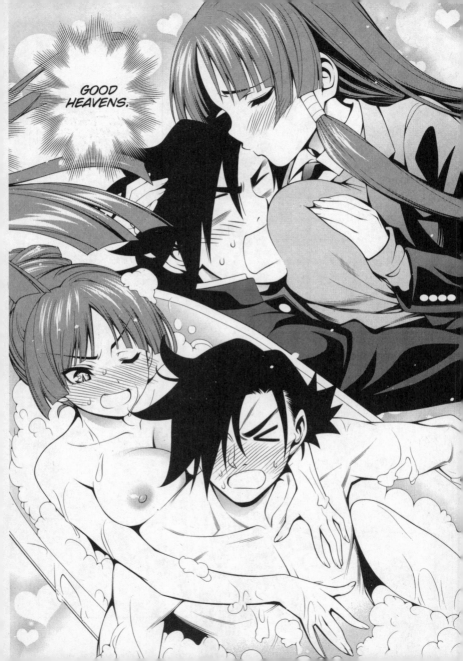

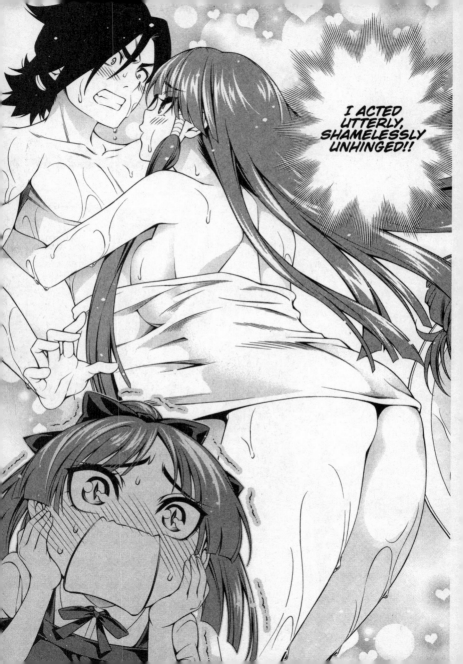

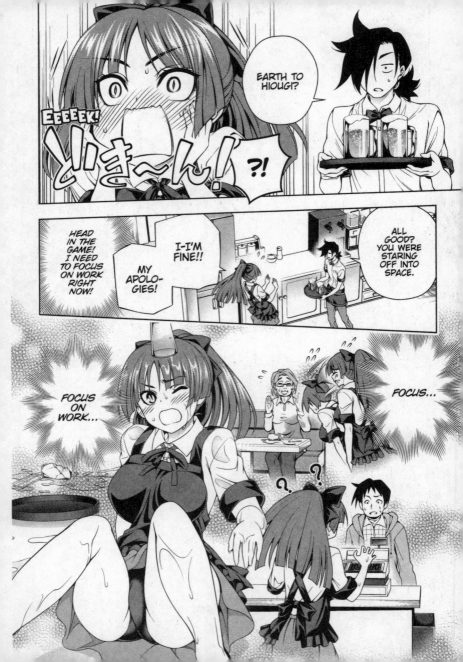

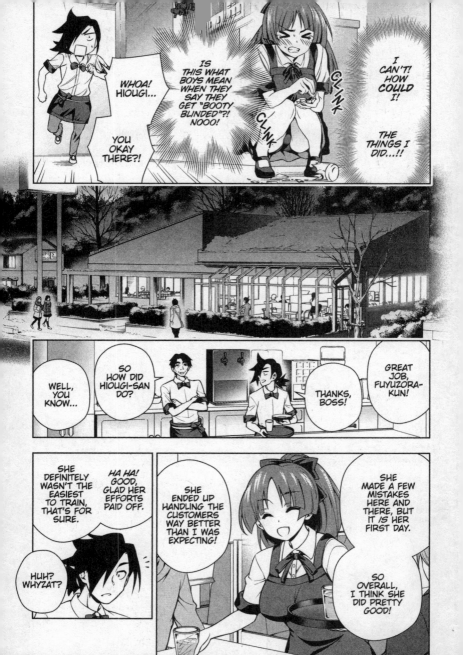

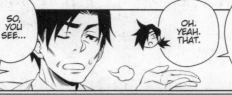

SOMETIMES THE WAY SHE TALKS AND ACTS CAN COME OFF A LITTLE... **PROUD,** YOU KNOW?

SO, YOU SEE...

OH. YEAH. THAT.

WELL, YOU KNOW HOW WELL OFF HIOUGI-SAN'S FAMILY IS, RIGHT...?

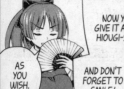

NOW YOU GIVE IT A TRY, HIOUGI-SAN!

AS YOU WISH.

AND DON'T FORGET TO SMILE!

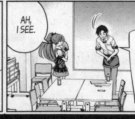

AH, I SEE.

FOLLOWED BY A QUICK BOW OF THE HEAD TO GREET THEM!

YOU SAY, "WELCOME!"

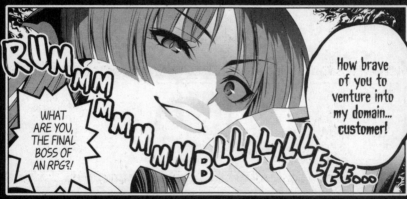

RUMMMMMMMMBLLLLLLLEEE...

WHAT ARE YOU, THE FINAL BOSS OF AN RPG?!

How brave of you to venture into my domain... customer!

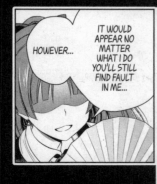

HOWEVER...

IT WOULD APPEAR NO MATTER WHAT I DO YOU'LL STILL FIND FAULT IN ME...

HUMPH, I'M AFRAID CANNED RESPONSES SUCH AS THOSE ARE NOT QUITE MY STYLE.

HOW MANY TIMES DO WE HAVE TO GO OVER THIS?!

A FRIENDLY GREETING IS THE FOUNDATION OF GOOD CUSTOMER SERVICE!

NO INTIMIDATING THE CUSTOMERS!!

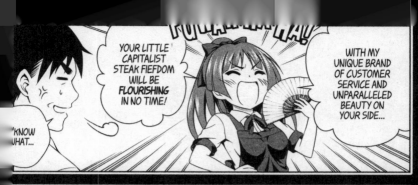
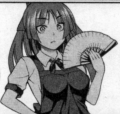
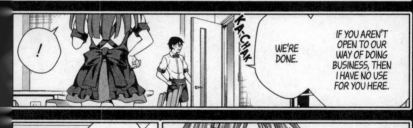
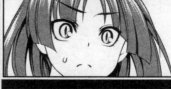
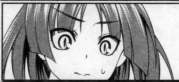
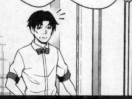

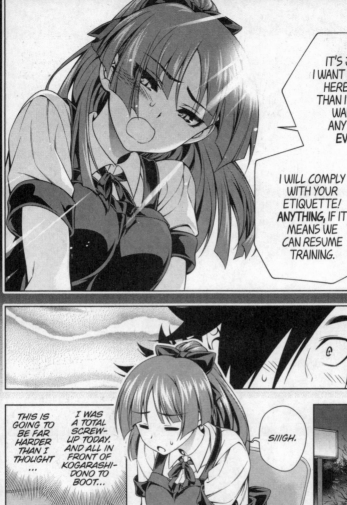

IT'S JUST...
I WANT TO WORK
HERE MORE
THAN I'VE EVER
WANTED
ANYTHING
EVER!!

I WILL COMPLY
WITH YOUR
ETIQUETTE!
ANYTHING, IF IT
MEANS WE
CAN RESUME
TRAINING.

THIS IS
GOING TO
BE FAR
HARDER
THAN I
THOUGHT
...

I WAS
A TOTAL
SCREW-
UP TODAY.
AND ALL IN
FRONT OF
KOGARASHI-
DONO TO
BOOT...

SIIIGH.

FWUMP

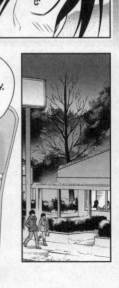

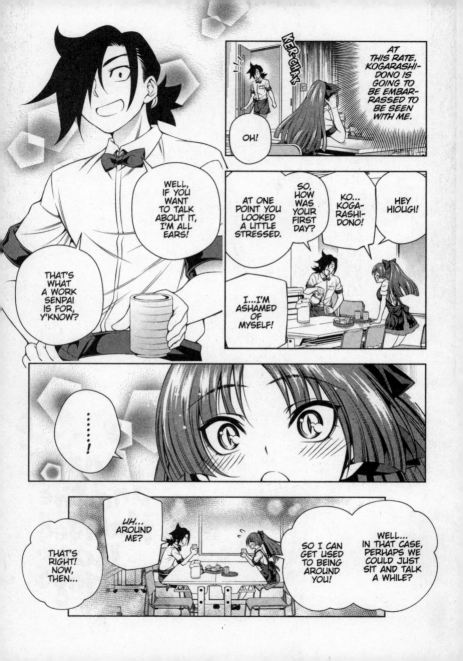

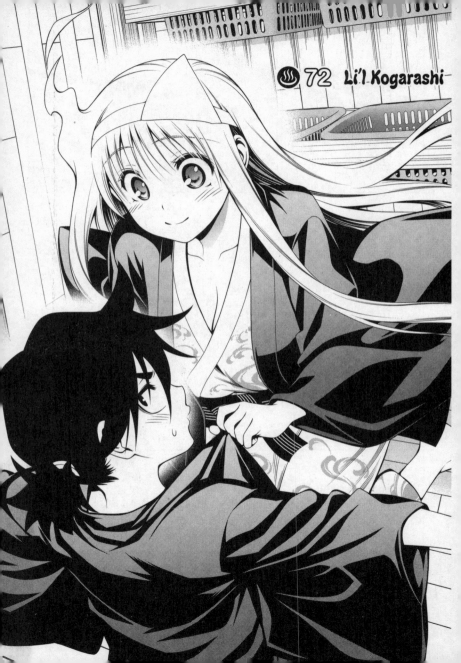

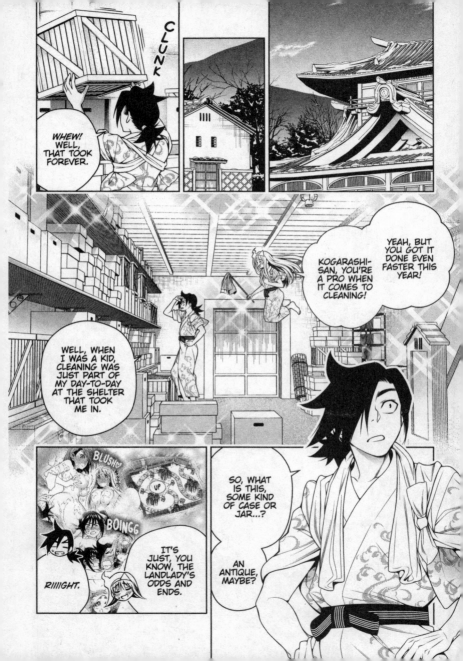

CLUNK

WHEW! WELL, THAT TOOK FOREVER.

KOGARASHI-SAN, YOU'RE A PRO WHEN IT COMES TO CLEANING!

YEAH, BUT YOU GOT IT DONE EVEN FASTER THIS YEAR!

WELL, WHEN I WAS A KID, CLEANING WAS JUST PART OF MY DAY-TO-DAY AT THE SHELTER THAT TOOK ME IN.

BLUSH

BOINGG

RIIIIGHT.

UP

IT'S JUST, YOU KNOW, THE LANDLADY'S ODDS AND ENDS.

SO, WHAT IS THIS, SOME KIND OF CASE OR JAR...?

AN ANTIQUE, MAYBE?

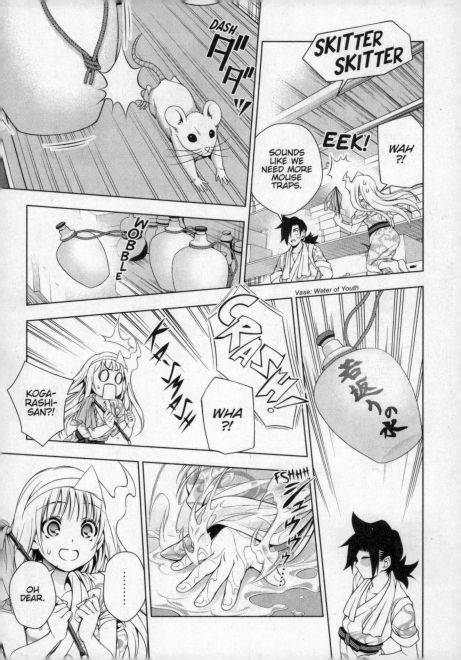

Vase: Water of Youth

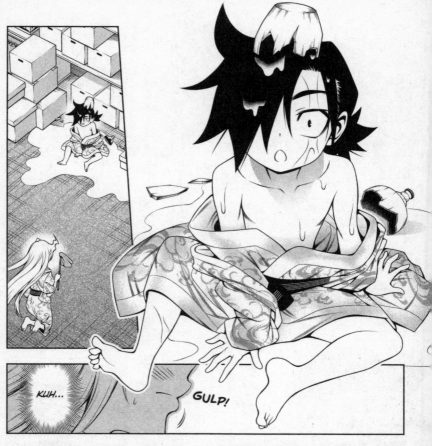

KUH...

GULP!

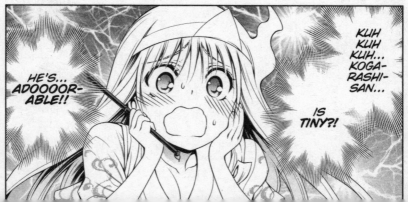

HE'S... ADOOOOR-ABLE!!

KUH KUH KUH... KOGA-RASHI-SAN...

IS TINY?!

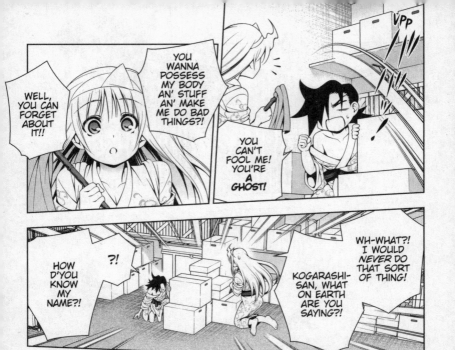

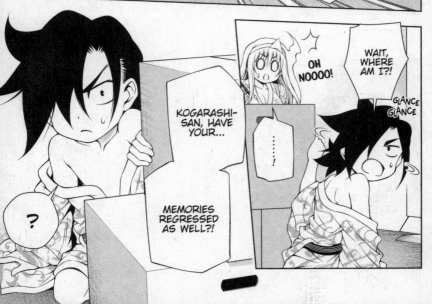

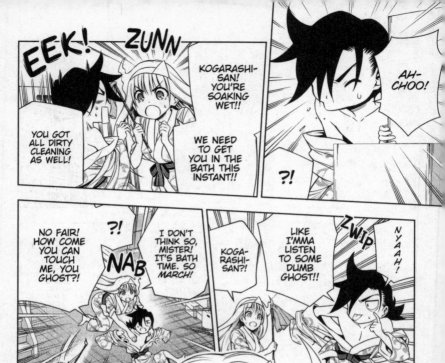

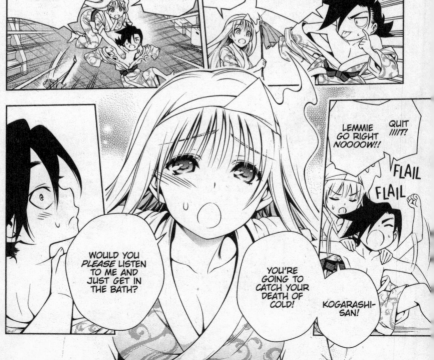

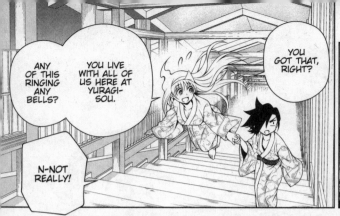

ANY OF THIS RINGING ANY BELLS?

YOU LIVE WITH ALL OF US HERE AT YURAGI-SOU.

YOU GOT THAT, RIGHT?

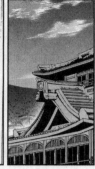

N-NOT REALLY!

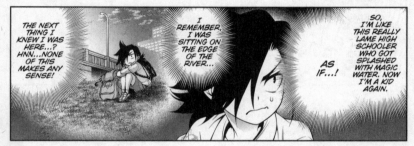

THE NEXT THING I KNEW I WAS HERE...? HNN...NONE OF THIS MAKES ANY SENSE!

I REMEMBER, I WAS SITTING ON THE EDGE OF THE RIVER...

AS IF...!

SO, I'M LIKE THIS REALLY LAME HIGH SCHOOLER WHO GOT SPLASHED WITH MAGIC WATER. NOW I'M A KID AGAIN.

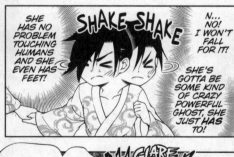

SHE HAS NO PROBLEM TOUCHING HUMANS AND SHE EVEN HAS FEET!

SHAKE SHAKE

N... NO! I WON'T FALL FOR IT!

SHE'S GOTTA BE SOME KIND OF CRAZY POWERFUL GHOST, SHE JUST HAS TO!

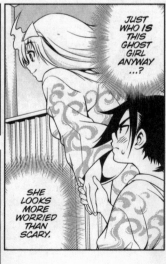

JUST WHO IS THIS GHOST GIRL ANYWAY ...?

SHE LOOKS MORE WORRIED THAN SCARY.

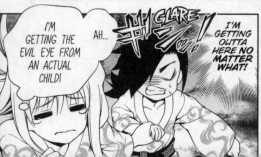

I'M GETTING THE EVIL EYE FROM AN ACTUAL CHILD!

AH...

GLARE

I'M GETTING OUTTA HERE NO MATTER WHAT!

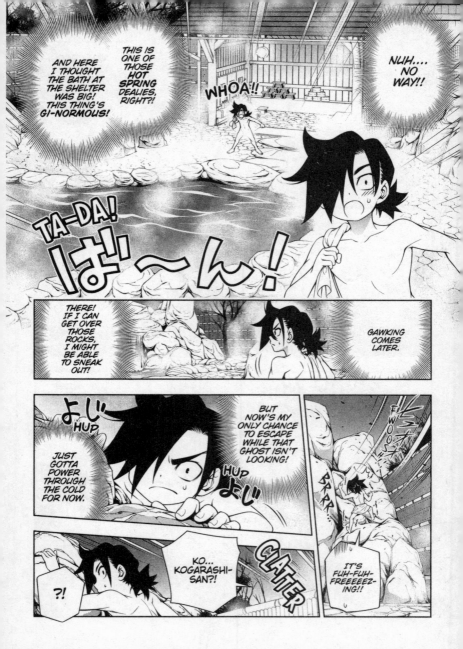

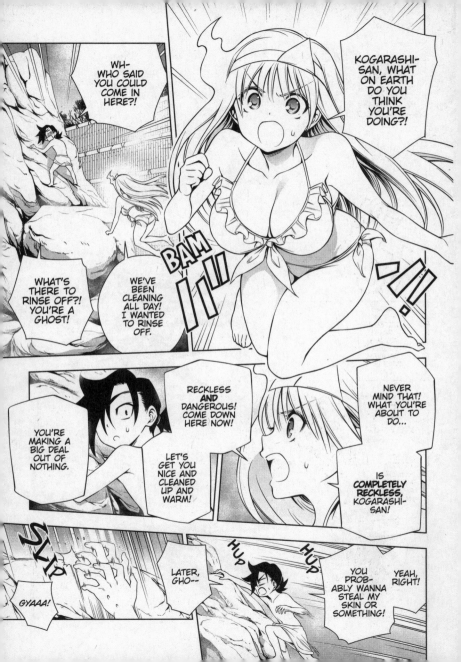

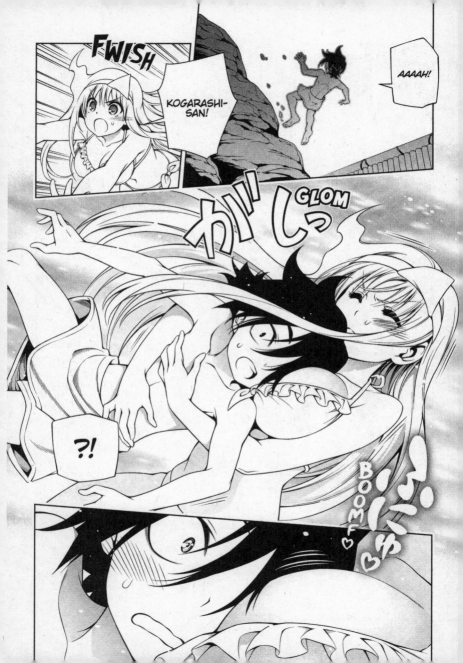

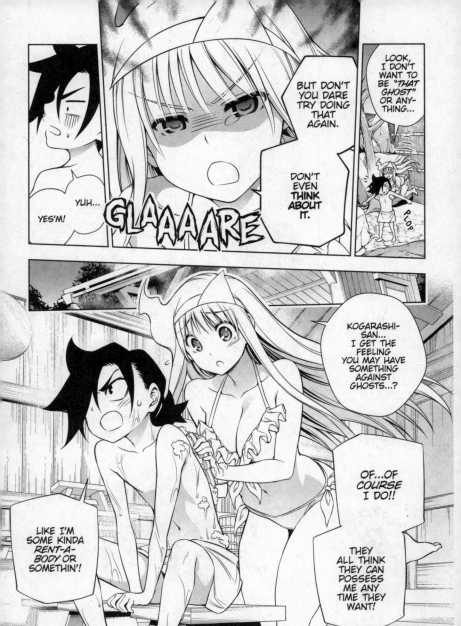

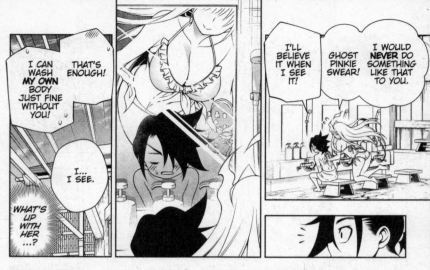

I CAN WASH **MY OWN** BODY JUST FINE WITHOUT YOU!

THAT'S ENOUGH!

I... I SEE.

WHAT'S UP WITH HER ...?

I'LL BELIEVE IT WHEN I SEE IT!

GHOST PINKIE SWEAR!

I WOULD **NEVER** DO SOMETHING LIKE THAT TO YOU.

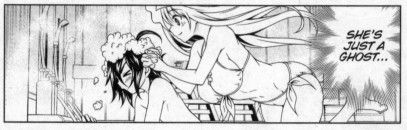

SHE'S JUST A GHOST...

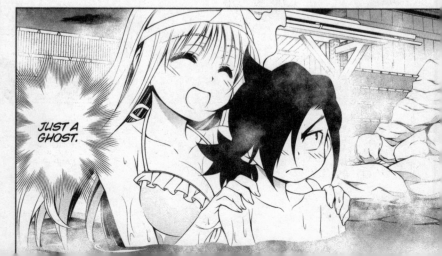

JUST A GHOST.

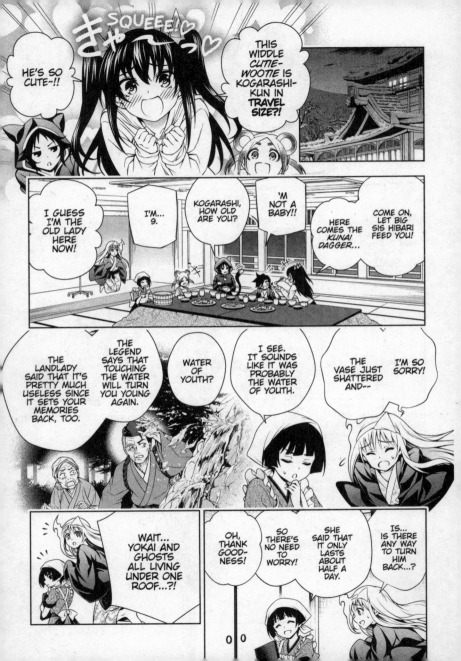

SQUEEE! ♡

HE'S SO CUTE~!!

THIS WIDDLE *CUTIE-WOOTIE* IS KOGARASHI-KUN IN TRAVEL SIZE?!

I GUESS I'M THE OLD LADY HERE NOW!

I'M... 9.

KOGARASHI, HOW OLD ARE YOU?

'M NOT A BABY!!

HERE COMES THE *KUNAI* DAGGER...

COME ON, LET BIG SIS HIBARI FEED YOU!

THE LANDLADY SAID THAT IT'S PRETTY MUCH USELESS SINCE IT SETS YOUR MEMORIES BACK, TOO.

THE LEGEND SAYS THAT TOUCHING THE WATER WILL TURN YOU YOUNG AGAIN.

WATER OF YOUTH?

I SEE. IT SOUNDS LIKE IT WAS PROBABLY THE WATER OF YOUTH.

THE VASE JUST SHATTERED AND--

I'M SO SORRY!

WAIT... YOKAI AND GHOSTS ALL LIVING UNDER ONE ROOF...?!

OH, THANK GOOD-NESS!

SO THERE'S NO NEED TO WORRY!

SHE SAID THAT IT ONLY LASTS ABOUT HALF A DAY.

IS... IS THERE ANY WAY TO TURN HIM BACK...?

0 0

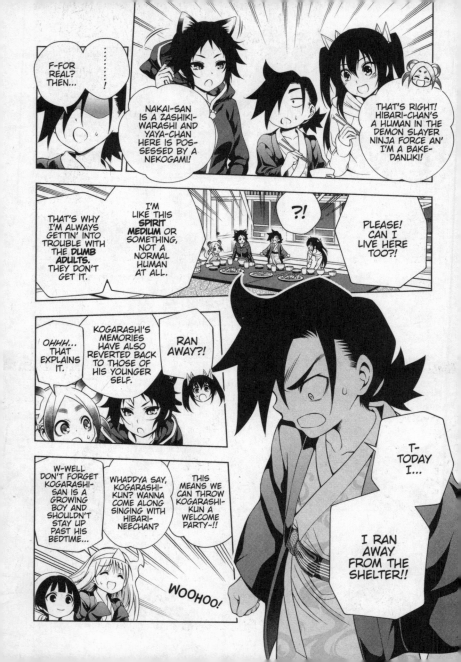

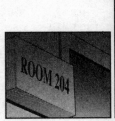

ROOM 204

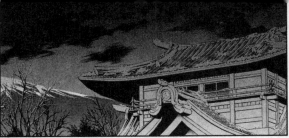

SMOOSH

ふよん

WHEN DID I FALL ASLEEP...?

I WAS AT DINNER AND...

HUH...?

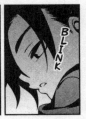

BLINK

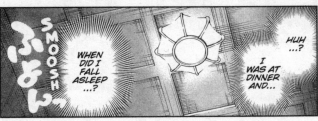

HMN...

GOOSH GOOSH

SO SOFT...

WHAZ-ZIS?

?

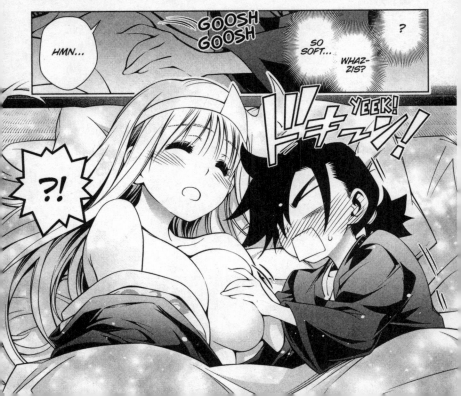

ドキューン!!

YEEK!

?!

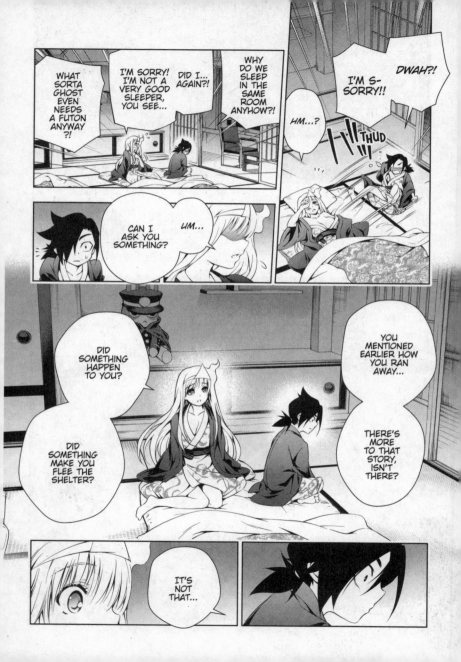

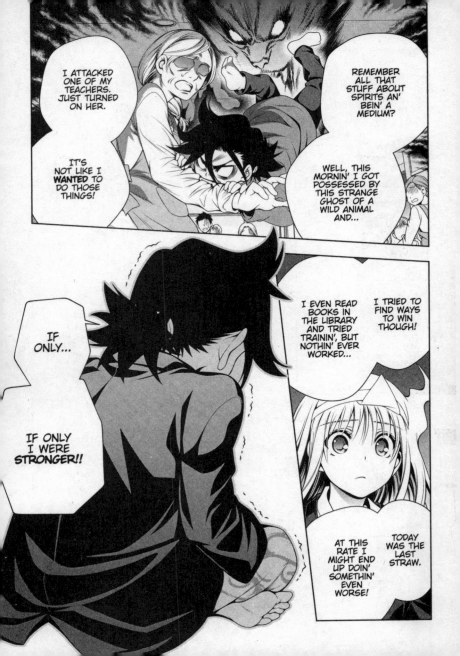

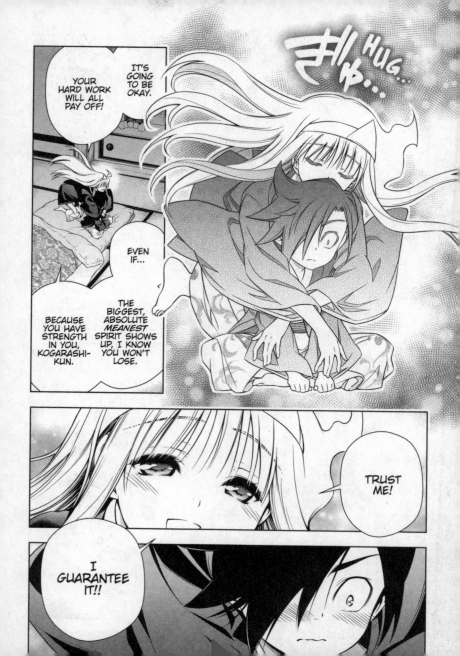

POOF! STRETCH

?!

SO... YOU REMEMBER EVERYTHING FROM YOUR EXPERIENCE?

WHO'DA THOUGHT I'D BECOME A KID, RIGHT?

SORRY 'BOUT THAT. GEEZ, I THINK I WAS A BIT OF A HANDFUL.

KOGA-RASHI-SAN, YOU...

WHERE DID YOU GO?

AFTER YOU RAN AWAY... WHAT DID YOU DO?

UMM...

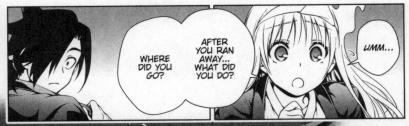

IT ALL TURNED OUT PRETTY GOOD IN THE END.

I GUESS I DID ALL SORTS OF DIFFERENT THINGS.

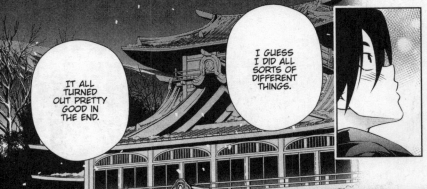

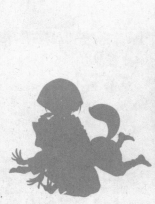

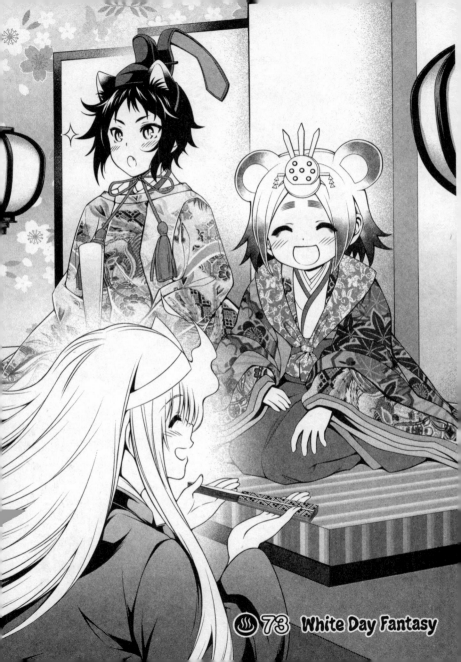

73 White Day Fantasy

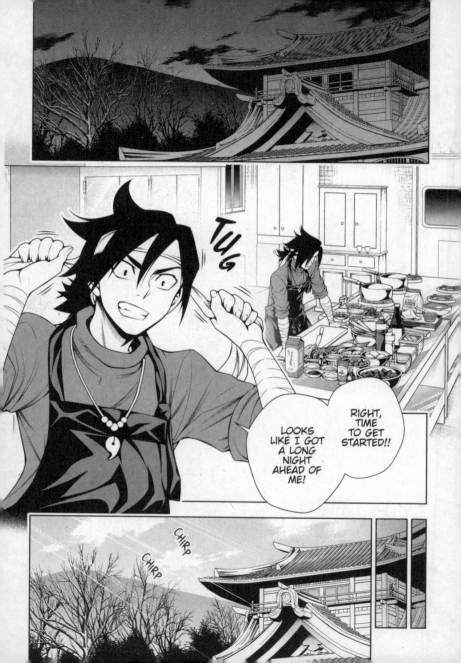

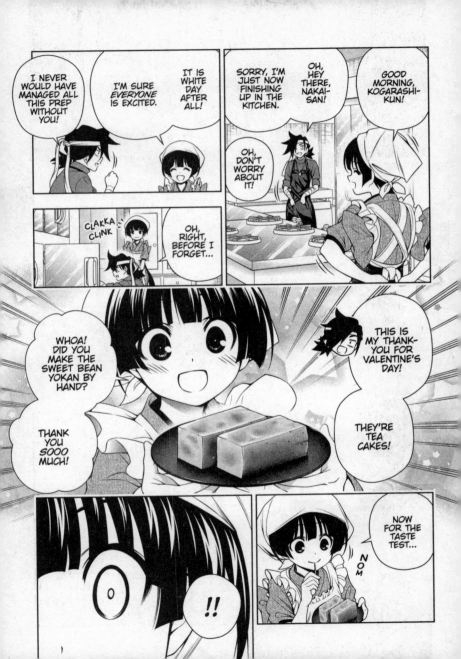

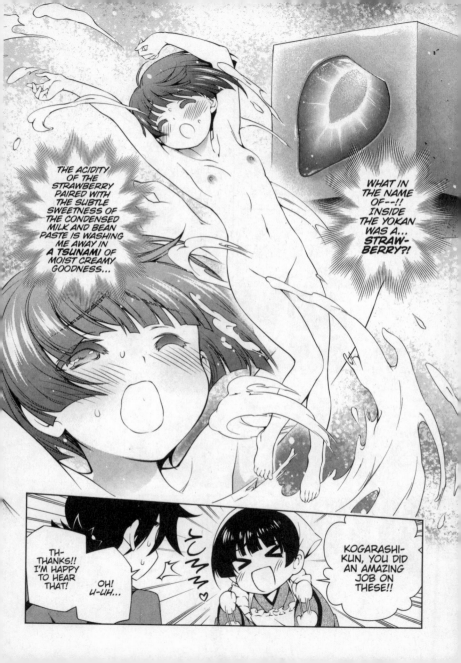

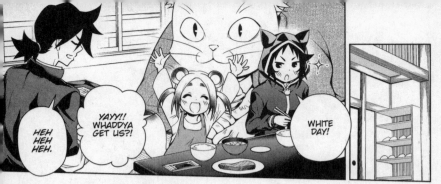

HEH HEH HEH.

YAYY!! WHADDYA GET US?!

WHITE DAY!

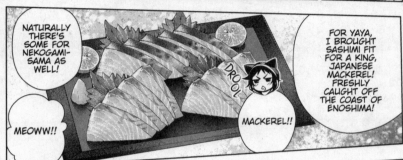

NATURALLY THERE'S SOME FOR NEKOGAMI-SAMA AS WELL!

MEOWW!!

DROOL

FOR YAYA, I BROUGHT SASHIMI FIT FOR A KING, JAPANESE MACKEREL! FRESHLY CAUGHT OFF THE COAST OF ENOSHIMA!

MACKEREL!!

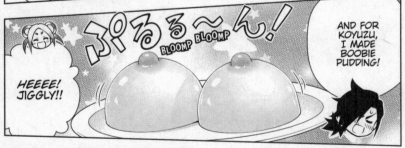

ぷるる〜ん！
BLOOMP BLOOMP

HEEEE! JIGGLY!!

AND FOR KOYUZU, I MADE BOOBIE PUDDING!

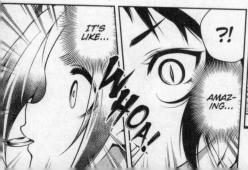

IT'S LIKE...

?!

WHOA!

AMAZING...

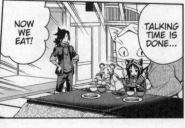

NOW WE EAT!

TALKING TIME IS DONE...

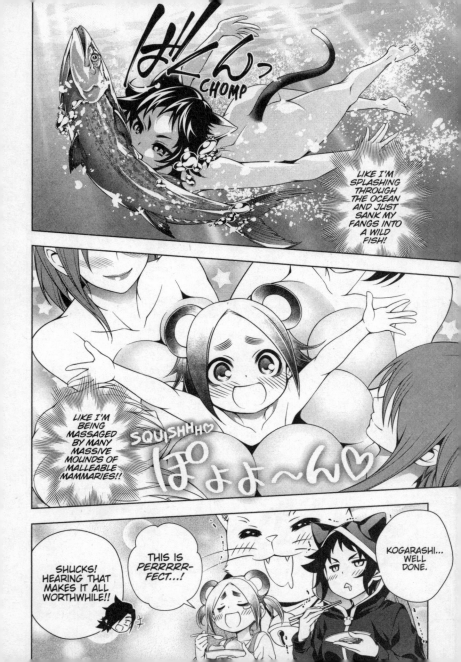

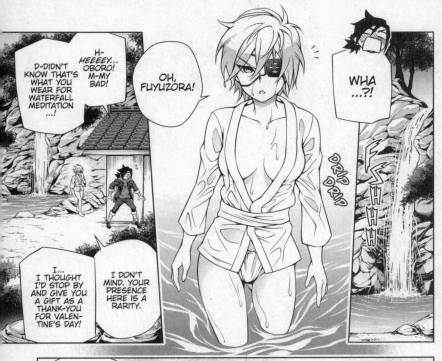

D-DIDN'T KNOW THAT'S WHAT YOU WEAR FOR WATERFALL MEDITATION ...!

H-HEEEEY... OBORO! M-MY BAD!

OH, FUYUZORA!

WHA ...?!

I... I THOUGHT I'D STOP BY AND GIVE YOU A GIFT AS A THANK-YOU FOR VALENTINE'S DAY!

I DON'T MIND. YOUR PRESENCE HERE IS A RARITY.

DRIP DRIP

FSHHHH

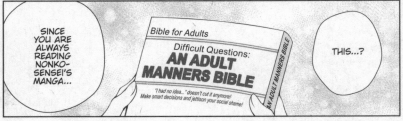

SINCE YOU ARE ALWAYS READING NONKO-SENSEI'S MANGA...

Bible for Adults

Difficult Questions:
AN ADULT MANNERS BIBLE

"I had no idea..." doesn't cut it anymore!
Make smart decisions and jettison your social shame!

AN ADULT MANNERS BIBLE

THIS...?

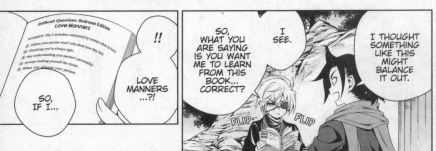

Difficult Questions: Bedroom Edition
Love Manners

WOMEN: The 5 mistakes committed by women when in love
① When your partner won't talk about how they feel.
② Thinking you're always right.
③ Not understanding your partner's personality.
④ Always making yourself the victim.
⑤ When you alienate your partner.

!!

SO, IF I...

LOVE MANNERS ...?!

SO, WHAT YOU ARE SAYING IS YOU WANT ME TO LEARN FROM THIS BOOK... CORRECT?

I SEE.

I THOUGHT SOMETHING LIKE THIS MIGHT BALANCE IT OUT.

FLIP

FLIP

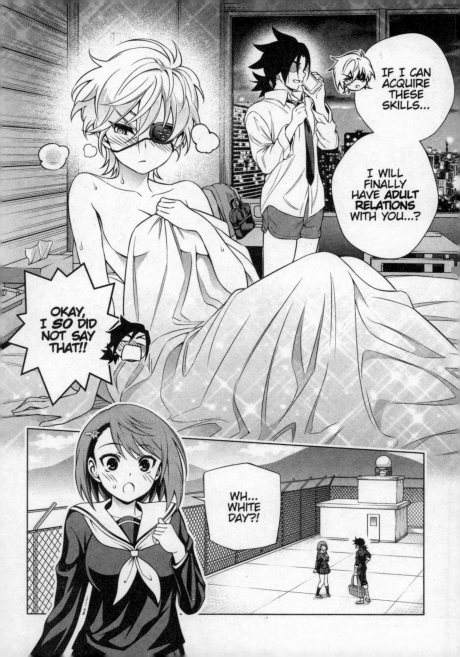

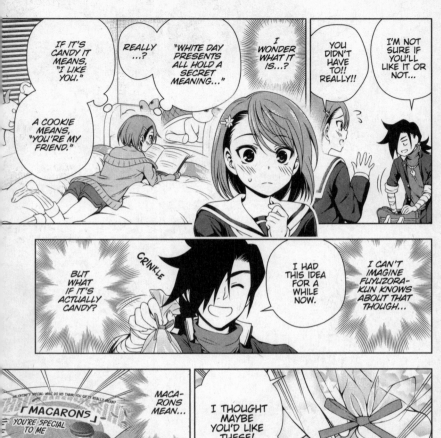

IF IT'S CANDY IT MEANS, "I LIKE YOU."

REALLY...?

"WHITE DAY PRESENTS ALL HOLD A SECRET MEANING..."

I WONDER WHAT IT IS...?

YOU DIDN'T HAVE TO!! REALLY!!

I'M NOT SURE IF YOU'LL LIKE IT OR NOT...

A COOKIE MEANS, "YOU'RE MY FRIEND."

GRINKLE

BUT WHAT IF IT'S ACTUALLY CANDY?

I HAD THIS IDEA FOR A WHILE NOW.

I CAN'T IMAGINE FUYUZORA-KUN KNOWS ABOUT THAT THOUGH...

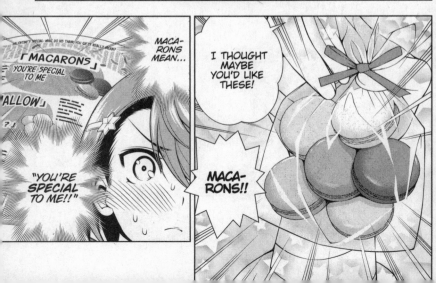

「MACARONS」 YOU'RE SPECIAL TO ME

「ALLOW」

MACA-RONS MEAN...

I THOUGHT MAYBE YOU'D LIKE THESE!

"YOU'RE SPECIAL TO ME!!"

MACA-RONS!!

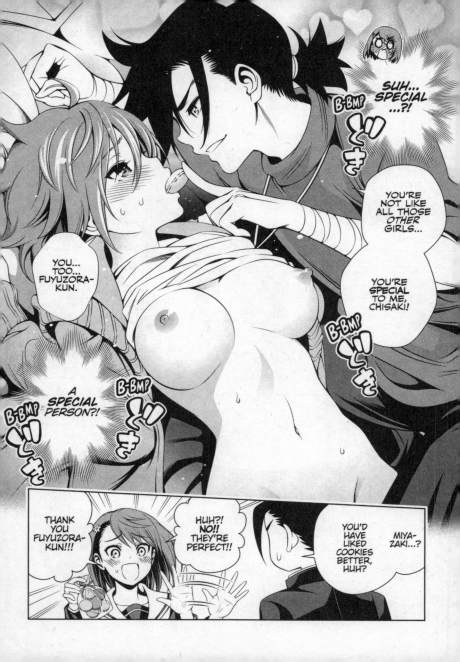

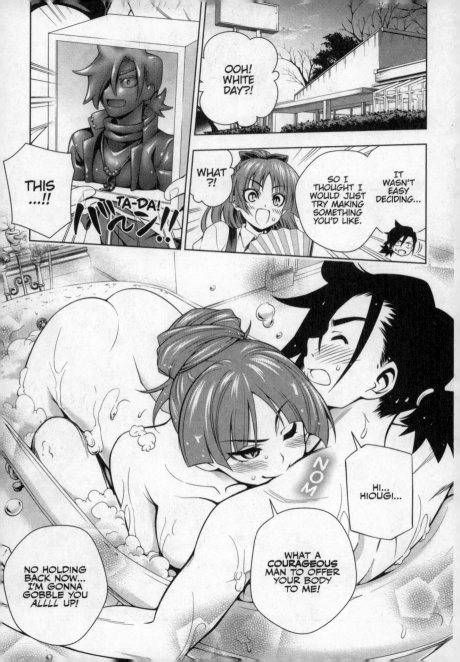

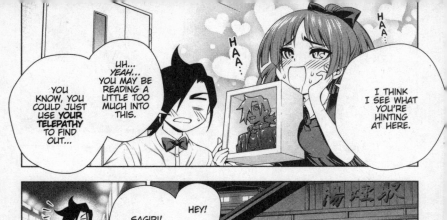

YOU KNOW, YOU COULD JUST USE **YOUR TELEPATHY** TO FIND OUT...

UH... YEAH... YOU MAY BE READING A LITTLE TOO MUCH INTO THIS.

HAA...

HAA...

I THINK I SEE WHAT YOU'RE HINTING AT HERE.

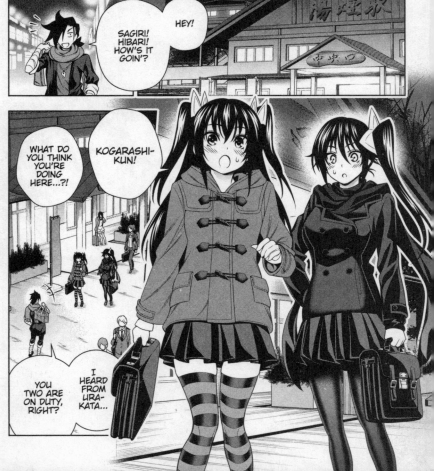

SAGIRI! HIBARI! HOW'S IT GOIN'?

HEY!

WHAT DO YOU THINK YOU'RE DOING HERE...?!

KOGARASHI-KUN!

YOU TWO ARE ON DUTY, RIGHT?

I HEARD FROM URA-KATA...

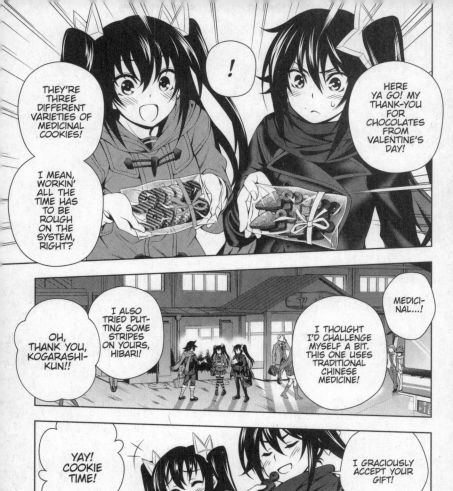

THEY'RE THREE DIFFERENT VARIETIES OF MEDICINAL COOKIES!

I MEAN, WORKIN' ALL THE TIME HAS TO BE ROUGH ON THE SYSTEM, RIGHT?

!

HERE YA GO! MY THANK-YOU FOR CHOCOLATES FROM VALENTINE'S DAY!

OH, THANK YOU, KOGARASHI-KUN!!

I ALSO TRIED PUTTING SOME STRIPES ON YOURS, HIBARI!

I THOUGHT I'D CHALLENGE MYSELF A BIT. THIS ONE USES TRADITIONAL CHINESE MEDICINE!

MEDICINAL...!

YAY! COOKIE TIME!

MUNCH

I GRACIOUSLY ACCEPT YOUR GIFT!

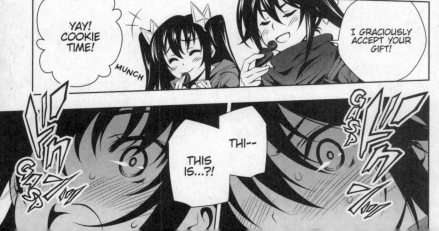

THI--

THIS IS...?!

GASP

GASP

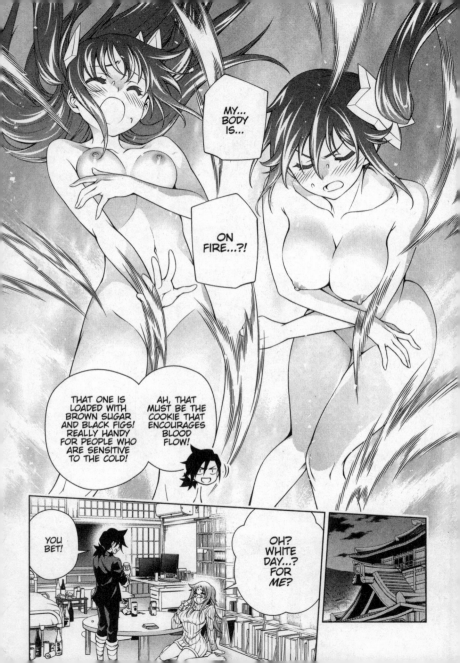

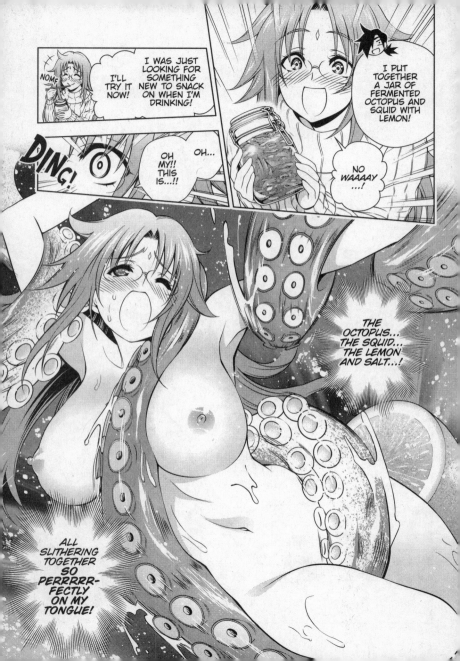

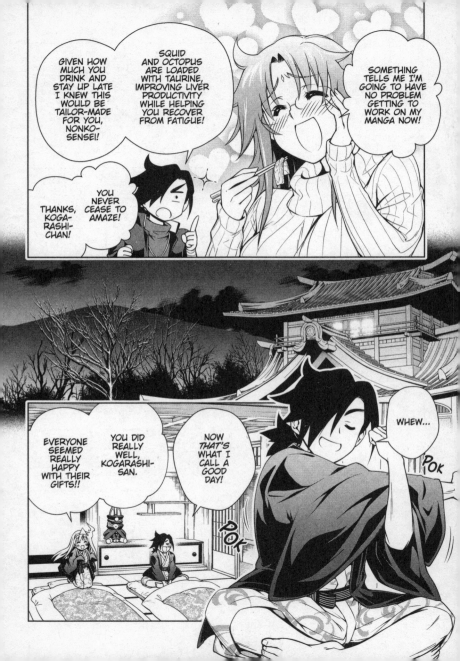

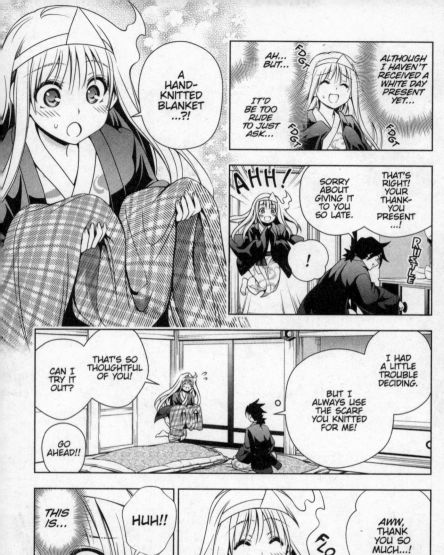

A HAND-KNITTED BLANKET...?!

AH... BUT...

IT'D BE TOO RUDE TO JUST ASK...

ALTHOUGH I HAVEN'T RECEIVED A WHITE DAY PRESENT YET...

FDGT

FDGT

FDGT

AHH!

SORRY ABOUT GIVING IT TO YOU SO LATE.

THAT'S RIGHT! YOUR THANK-YOU PRESENT...!

!

RUSTLE

CAN I TRY IT OUT?

THAT'S SO THOUGHTFUL OF YOU!

I HAD A LITTLE TROUBLE DECIDING.

BUT I ALWAYS USE THE SCARF YOU KNITTED FOR ME!

GO AHEAD!!

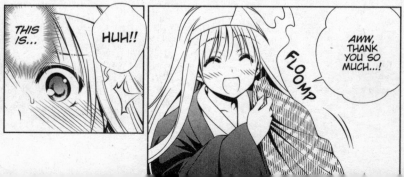

THIS IS...

HUH!!

AWW, THANK YOU SO MUCH...!

FLOOMP

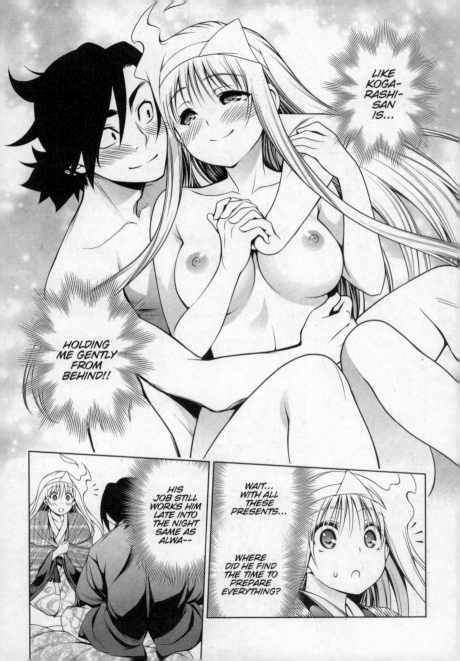

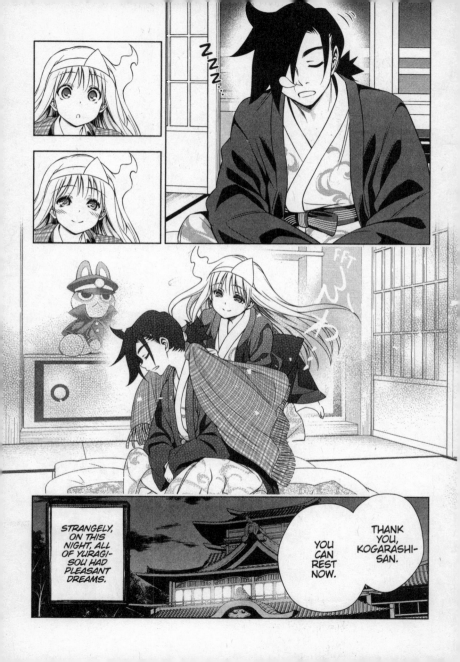

ZZZ...

FFT...

STRANGELY, ON THIS NIGHT, ALL OF YURAGI-SOU HAD PLEASANT DREAMS.

YOU CAN REST NOW.

THANK YOU, KOGARASHI-SAN.

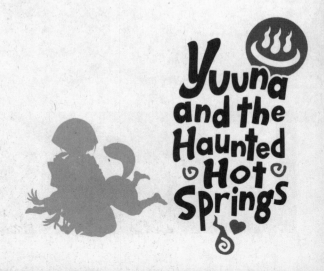

Yuuna
and the
Haunted
Hot
Springs

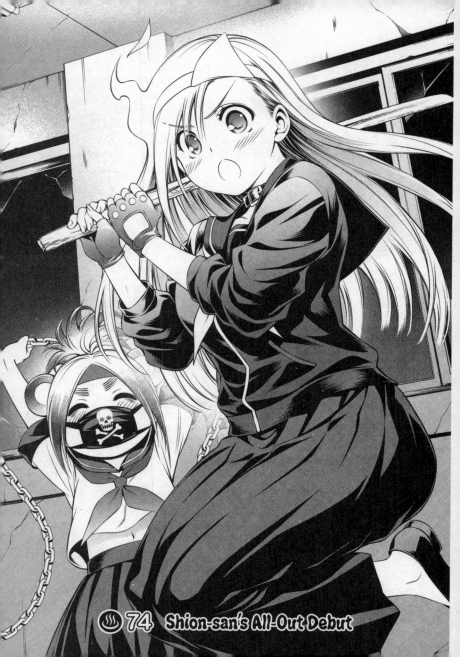

74 Shion-san's All-Out Debut

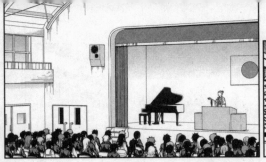

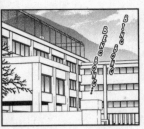

BING BONG... BING BONG...

REALLY? WHYZZAT?

SERIOUSLY CAN'T WAIT, FUYUZORA!

FINALLY! WE'RE GOING TO BE SECOND YEAR STUDENTS! OUR TIME HAS COME!

WELLLL... I WOULDN'T MIND GOING ON A DAY TRIP SOMEWHERE!

SPRING BREAK STARTS TOMORROW! YOU GOT ANY PLANS, YUUNA?

CHATTER

WAIT... YOU **DON'T KNOW?!** AS SECOND YEAR STUDENTS...

CHATTER

CHATTER

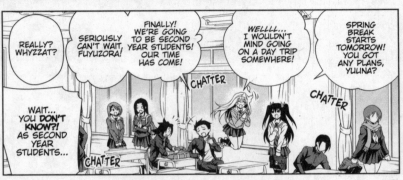

YOU HAVE A ONE TRACK MIND, HYOUDOU.

THE CUTE-AS-A-BUTTON NEW KOUHAI WILL *OH-SO-ADORABLY* SAY TO ME!!

"HYOUDOU-SENPAAAA!! ♡"

WE'LL GET TO HAVE KOUHAI!!

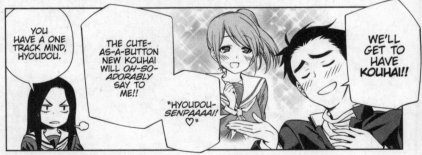

?

WHAT KIND OF SOME-ONE?

THERE'S SOMEONE I WANT YOU TO MEET!

YOU GOT ANY FREE TIME THIS WEEK?

THAT'S RIGHT! CHISAKI!

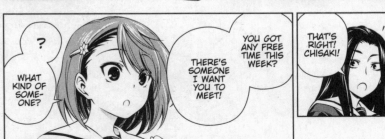

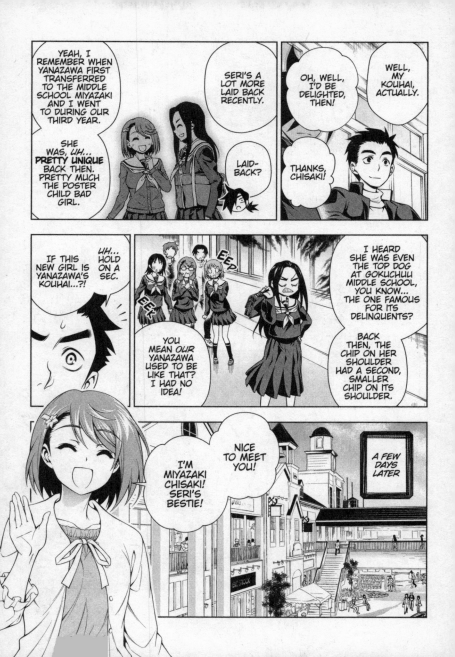

YEAH, I REMEMBER WHEN YANAZAWA FIRST TRANSFERRED TO THE MIDDLE SCHOOL MIYAZAKI AND I WENT TO DURING OUR THIRD YEAR.

SHE WAS, *UH...* **PRETTY UNIQUE** BACK THEN. PRETTY MUCH THE POSTER CHILD BAD GIRL.

SERI'S A LOT MORE LAID BACK RECENTLY.

LAID-BACK?

OH, WELL, I'D BE DELIGHTED, THEN!

WELL, MY KOUHAI, ACTUALLY.

THANKS, CHISAKI!

IF THIS NEW GIRL IS YANAZAWA'S KOUHAI...?!

UH... HOLD ON A SEC.

EEP

EEP

I HEARD SHE WAS EVEN THE TOP DOG AT GOKUCHUU MIDDLE SCHOOL, YOU KNOW... THE ONE FAMOUS FOR ITS DELINQUENTS?

YOU MEAN *OUR* YANAZAWA USED TO BE LIKE THAT? I HAD NO IDEA!

BACK THEN, THE CHIP ON HER SHOULDER HAD A SECOND, SMALLER CHIP ON ITS SHOULDER.

NICE TO MEET YOU!

I'M MIYAZAKI CHISAKI! SERI'S BESTIE!

A FEW DAYS LATER

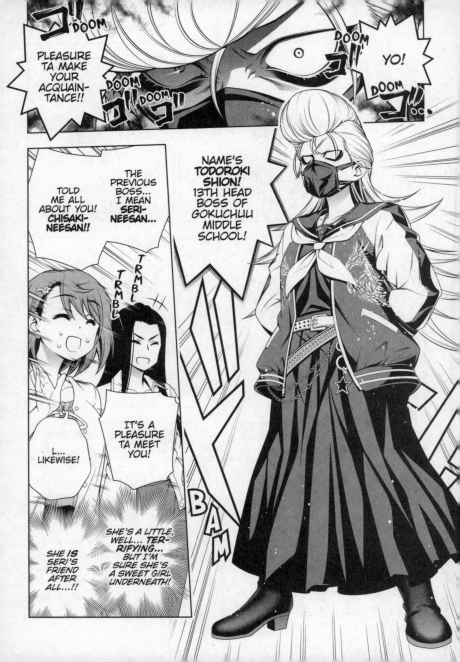

GO!! DOOM

PLEASURE TA MAKE YOUR ACQUAIN-TANCE!!

DOOM!! GO

DOOM!! GO

DOOM!! GO

YO!

DOOM!! GO...

NAME'S TODOROKI SHION! 13TH HEAD BOSS OF GOKUCHUU MIDDLE SCHOOL!

TOLD ME ALL ABOUT YOU! CHISAKI-NEESAN!!

THE PREVIOUS BOSS... I MEAN SERI-NEESAN...

TRMBL

TRMBL

IT'S A PLEASURE TA MEET YOU!

L... LIKEWISE!

BAM

SHE IS SERI'S FRIEND AFTER ALL...!!

SHE'S A LITTLE, WELL... TER-RIFYING... BUT I'M SURE SHE'S A SWEET GIRL UNDERNEATH!

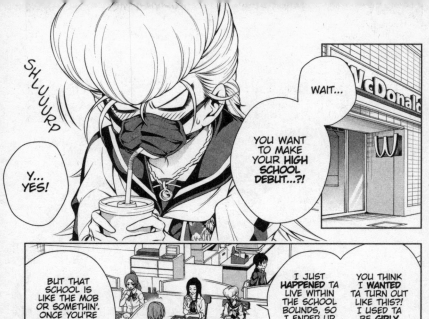

SHLUUURP

WAIT...

YOU WANT TO MAKE YOUR **HIGH SCHOOL DEBUT**...?!

Y... YES!

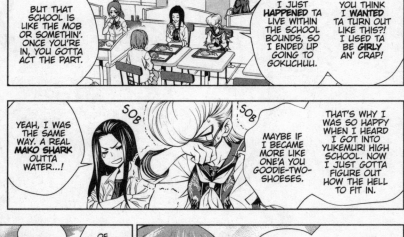

BUT THAT SCHOOL IS LIKE THE MOB OR SOMETHIN'. ONCE YOU'RE IN, YOU GOTTA ACT THE PART.

I JUST **HAPPENED** TA LIVE WITHIN THE SCHOOL BOUNDS, SO I ENDED UP GOING TO GOKUCHUU.

YOU THINK I **WANTED** TA TURN OUT LIKE THIS?! I USED TA BE **GIRLY** AN' CRAP!

YEAH, I WAS THE SAME WAY. A REAL **MAKO SHARK** OUTTA WATER...!

SOB

SOB

MAYBE IF I BECAME MORE LIKE ONE'A YOU GOODIE-TWO-SHOESES.

THAT'S WHY I WAS SO HAPPY WHEN I HEARD I GOT INTO YUKEMURI HIGH SCHOOL. NOW I JUST GOTTA FIGURE OUT HOW THE HELL TO FIT IN.

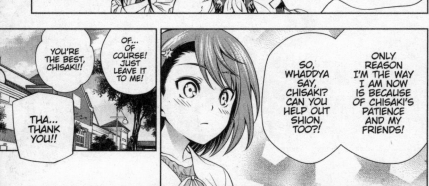

YOU'RE THE BEST, CHISAKI!!

OF... OF COURSE! JUST LEAVE IT TO ME!

THA... THANK YOU!!

SO, WHADDYA SAY, CHISAKI? CAN YOU HELP OUT SHION, TOO?!

ONLY REASON I'M THE WAY I AM NOW IS BECAUSE OF CHISAKI'S PATIENCE AND MY FRIENDS!

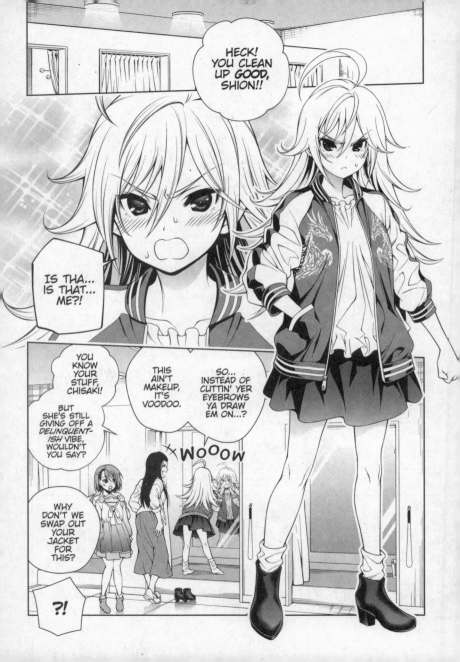

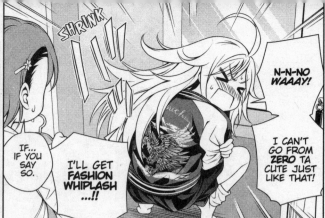

SHRINK

N-N-NO WAAAY!

I CAN'T GO FROM ZERO TA CUTE JUST LIKE THAT!

IF... IF YOU SAY SO.

I'LL GET FASHION WHIPLASH ...!!

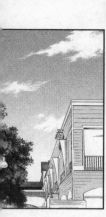

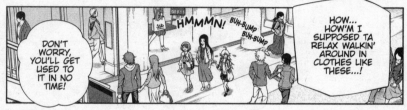

DON'T WORRY, YOU'LL GET USED TO IT IN NO TIME!

HMMMN!

BUH-BUMP BUH-BUMP

HOW... HOW'M I SUPPOSED TA RELAX WALKIN' AROUND IN CLOTHES LIKE THESE...!

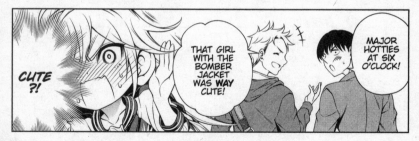

CUTE ?!

THAT GIRL WITH THE BOMBER JACKET WAS WAY CUTE!

MAJOR HOTTIES AT SIX O'CLOCK!

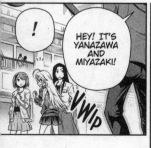

!

HEY! IT'S YANAZAWA AND MIYAZAKI!

VWIp

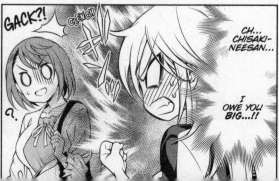

GACK?!

CLENCH

?

CH... CHISAKI-NEESAN...

I OWE YOU BIG...!!

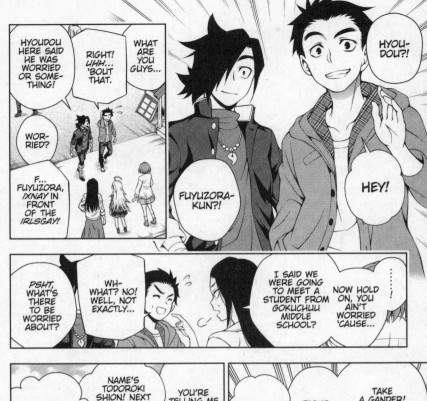

HYOUDOU HERE SAID HE WAS WORRIED OR SOMETHING!

RIGHT! UHH... 'BOUT THAT.

WHAT ARE YOU GUYS...

HYOUDOU?!

WORRIED?

F... FUYUZORA, IXNAY IN FRONT OF THE IRLSGAY!

FUYUZORA-KUN?!

HEY!

PSHT, WHAT'S THERE TO BE WORRIED ABOUT?

WH-WHAT? NO! WELL, NOT EXACTLY...

I SAID WE WERE GOING TO MEET A STUDENT FROM GOKUCHUU MIDDLE SCHOOL?

NOW HOLD ON, YOU AIN'T WORRIED 'CAUSE...

!

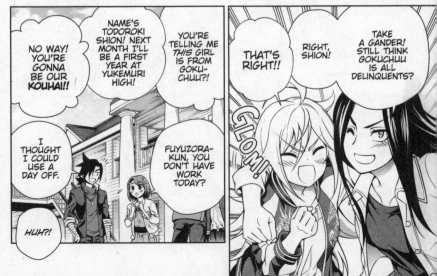

NO WAY! YOU'RE GONNA BE OUR KOUHAI!!

NAME'S TODOROKI SHION! NEXT MONTH I'LL BE A FIRST YEAR AT YUKEMURI HIGH!

YOU'RE TELLING ME THIS GIRL IS FROM GOKU-CHUU?!

THAT'S RIGHT!!

RIGHT, SHION!

TAKE A GANDER! STILL THINK GOKUCHUU IS ALL DELINQUENTS?

I THOUGHT I COULD USE A DAY OFF.

FUYUZORA-KUN, YOU DON'T HAVE WORK TODAY?

HUH?!

GLOM!

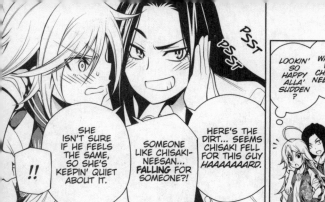

PSST
PSST

!!

SHE ISN'T SURE IF HE FEELS THE SAME, SO SHE'S KEEPIN' QUIET ABOUT IT.

SOMEONE LIKE CHISAKI-NEESAN... **FALLING** FOR SOMEONE?!

HERE'S THE DIRT... SEEMS CHISAKI FELL FOR THIS GUY HAAAAAAARD.

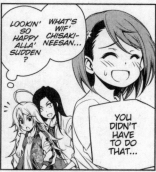

LOOKIN' SO HAPPY ALLA' SUDDEN?

WHAT'S WIF' CHISAKI-NEESAN...

YOU DIDN'T HAVE TO DO THAT...

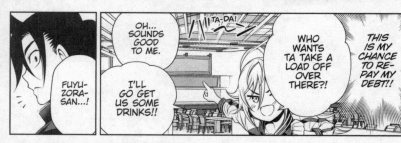

OH... SOUNDS GOOD TO ME.

FUYU-ZORA-SAN...!

I'LL GO GET US SOME DRINKS!!

TA-DA!

WHO WANTS TA TAKE A LOAD OFF OVER THERE?!

THIS IS MY CHANCE TO RE-PAY MY DEBT!!

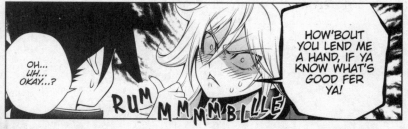

OH... UH... OKAY...?

HOW'BOUT YOU LEND ME A HAND, IF YA KNOW WHAT'S GOOD FER YA!

RUMMMMMBLLLE

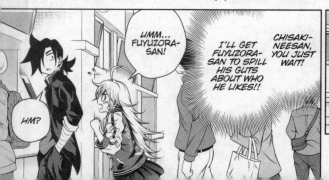

UMM... FUYUZORA-SAN!

I'LL GET FUYUZORA-SAN TO SPILL HIS GUTS ABOUT WHO HE LIKES!!

CHISAKI-NEESAN, YOU JUST WAIT!

HM?

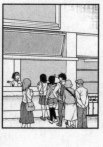

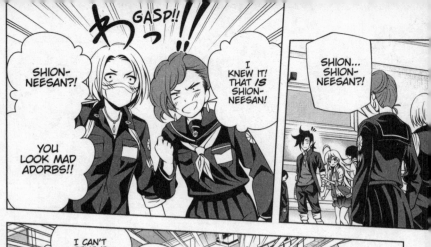

GASP!!!!

SHION-NEESAN?!

YOU LOOK MAD ADORBS!!

I KNEW IT! THAT *IS* SHION-NEESAN!

SHION... SHION-NEESAN?!

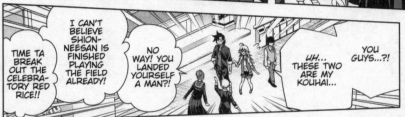

TIME TA BREAK OUT THE CELEBRATORY RED RICE!!

I CAN'T BELIEVE SHION-NEESAN IS FINISHED PLAYING THE FIELD ALREADY!

NO WAY! YOU LANDED YOURSELF A MAN?!

UH... THESE TWO ARE MY KOUHAI...

YOU GUYS...?!

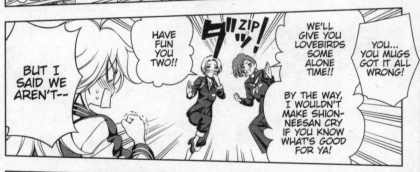

BUT I SAID WE AREN'T--

ZIP!

HAVE FUN YOU TWO!!

WE'LL GIVE YOU LOVEBIRDS SOME ALONE TIME!!

YOU... YOU MUGS GOT IT ALL WRONG!

BY THE WAY, I WOULDN'T MAKE SHION-NEESAN CRY IF YOU KNOW WHAT'S GOOD FOR YA!

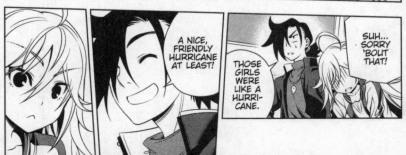

A NICE, FRIENDLY HURRICANE AT LEAST!

THOSE GIRLS WERE LIKE A HURRICANE.

SUH... SORRY 'BOUT THAT!

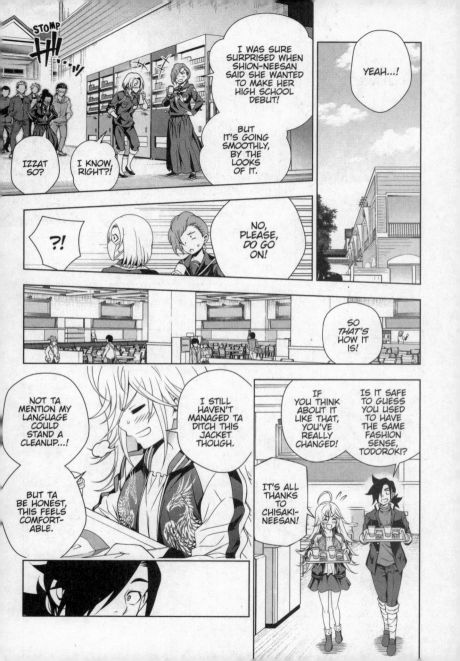

STOMP

I WAS SURE SURPRISED WHEN SHION-NEESAN SAID SHE WANTED TO MAKE HER HIGH SCHOOL DEBUT!

YEAH...!

BUT IT'S GOING SMOOTHLY, BY THE LOOKS OF IT.

IZZAT SO?

I KNOW, RIGHT?!

?!

NO, PLEASE, DO GO ON!

SO *THAT'S* HOW IT IS!

NOT TA MENTION MY LANGUAGE COULD STAND A CLEANUP...!

I STILL HAVEN'T MANAGED TA DITCH THIS JACKET THOUGH.

IF YOU THINK ABOUT IT LIKE THAT, YOU'VE REALLY CHANGED!

IS IT SAFE TO GUESS YOU USED TO HAVE THE SAME FASHION SENSE, TODOROKI?

BUT TA BE HONEST, THIS FEELS COMFORTABLE.

IT'S ALL THANKS TO CHISAKI-NEESAN!

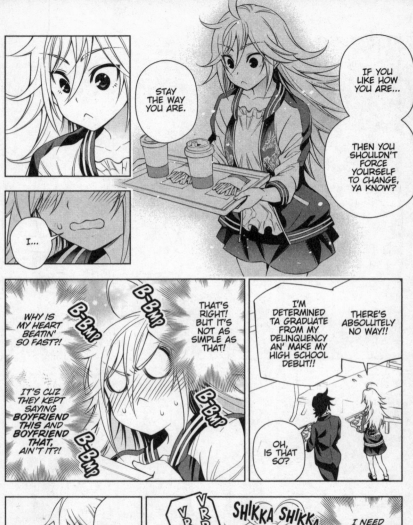

STAY THE WAY YOU ARE.

IF YOU LIKE HOW YOU ARE...

THEN YOU SHOULDN'T FORCE YOURSELF TO CHANGE, YA KNOW?

I...

WHY IS MY HEART BEATIN' SO FAST?!

B-BMP

B-BMP

B-BMP

B-BMP

B-BMP

IT'S CUZ THEY KEPT SAYING BOYFRIEND THIS AND BOYFRIEND THAT, AIN'T IT?!

THAT'S RIGHT! BUT IT'S NOT AS SIMPLE AS THAT!

I'M DETERMINED TA GRADUATE FROM MY DELINQUENCY AN' MAKE MY HIGH SCHOOL DEBUT!!

THERE'S ABSOLUTELY NO WAY!!

OH, IS THAT SO?

WHAT'S THIS?

VRRR VRRR

SHIKKA SHIKKA

!

I NEED TA STOP! CHISAKI-NEESAN IS THE ONE WHO LIKES FUYUZORA-SAN!!

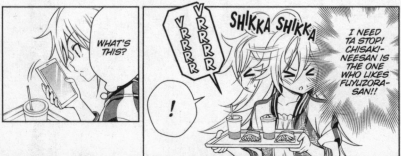

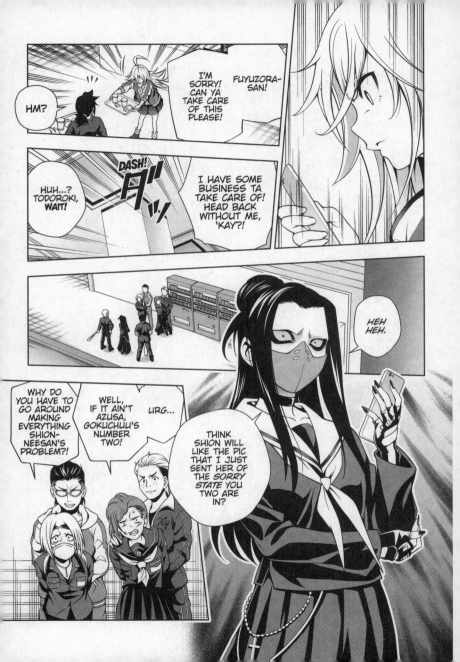

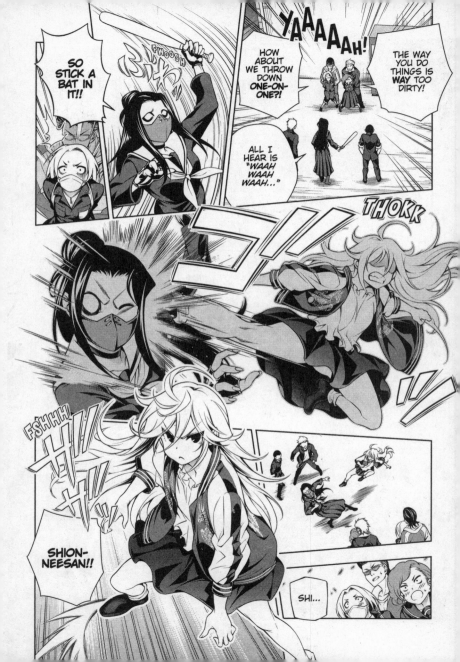

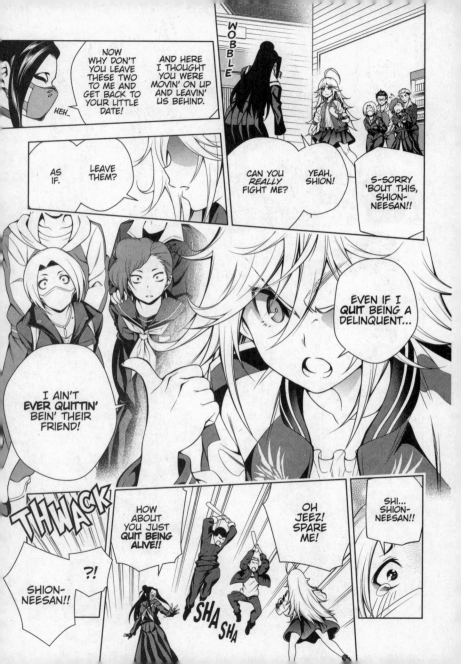

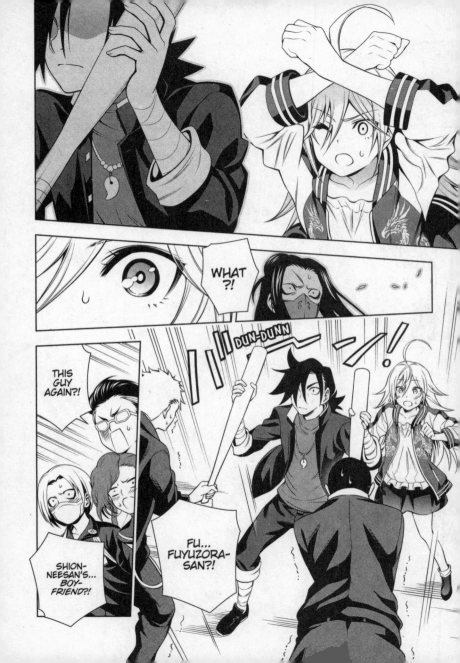

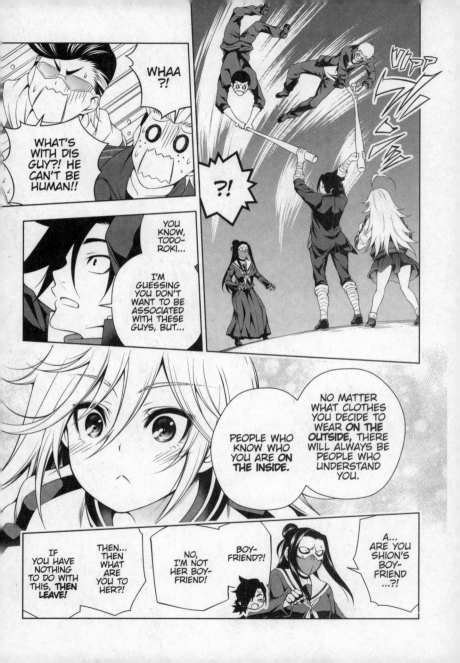

WHAA?!

WHAT'S WITH DIS GUY?! HE CAN'T BE HUMAN!!

?!

YOU KNOW, TODO-ROKI...

I'M GUESSING YOU DON'T WANT TO BE ASSOCIATED WITH THESE GUYS, BUT...

NO MATTER WHAT CLOTHES YOU DECIDE TO WEAR **ON THE OUTSIDE,** THERE WILL ALWAYS BE PEOPLE WHO UNDERSTAND YOU.

PEOPLE WHO KNOW WHO YOU ARE **ON THE INSIDE.**

IF YOU HAVE NOTHING TO DO WITH THIS, **THEN LEAVE!**

THEN... THEN WHAT ARE YOU TO HER?!

NO, I'M NOT HER BOY-FRIEND!

BOY-FRIEND?!

A... ARE YOU SHION'S BOY-FRIEND...?!

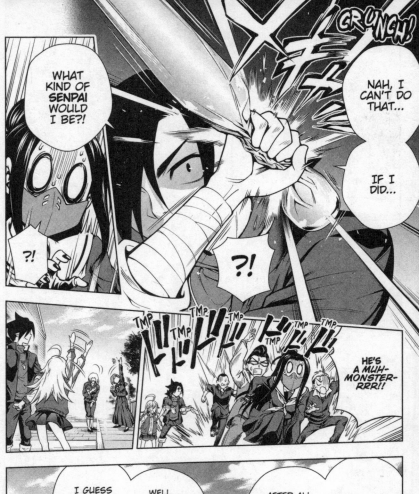

CRUNCH!

WHAT KIND OF SENPAI WOULD I BE?!

NAH, I CAN'T DO THAT...

IF I DID...

?!

?!

TMP TMP TMP TMP TMP TMP

HE'S A MUH- MONSTER- RRR!!

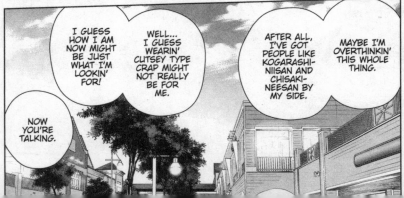

I GUESS HOW I AM NOW MIGHT BE JUST WHAT I'M LOOKIN' FOR!

WELL... I GUESS WEARIN' CUTSEY TYPE CRAP MIGHT NOT REALLY BE FOR ME.

AFTER ALL, I'VE GOT PEOPLE LIKE KOGARASHI- NIISAN AND CHISAKI- NEESAN BY MY SIDE.

MAYBE I'M OVERTHINKIN' THIS WHOLE THING.

NOW YOU'RE TALKING.

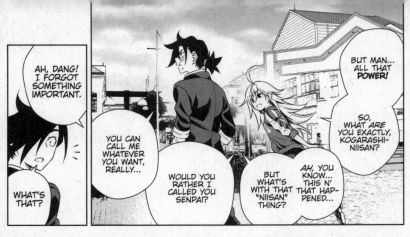

AH, DANG! I FORGOT SOMETHING IMPORTANT.

BUT MAN... ALL THAT **POWER!**

SO, WHAT ARE YOU EXACTLY, KOGARASHI-NIISAN?

YOU CAN CALL ME WHATEVER YOU WANT, REALLY...

WOULD YOU RATHER I CALLED YOU SENPAI?

BUT WHAT'S WITH THAT "NIISAN" THING?

AH, YOU KNOW... THIS N' THAT HAPPENED...

WHAT'S THAT?

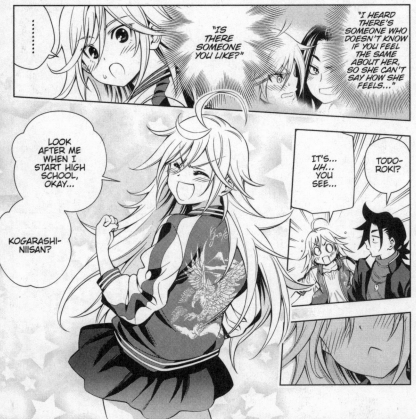

· · · · · ·

"IS THERE SOMEONE YOU LIKE?"

"I HEARD THERE'S SOMEONE WHO DOESN'T KNOW IF YOU FEEL THE SAME ABOUT HER, SO SHE CAN'T SAY HOW SHE FEELS..."

LOOK AFTER ME WHEN I START HIGH SCHOOL, OKAY...

IT'S... UH... YOU SEE...

TODO-ROKI?

KOGARASHI-NIISAN?

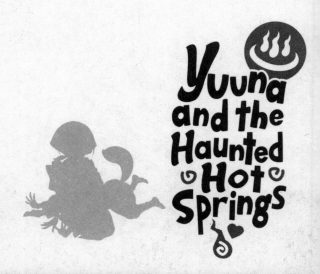

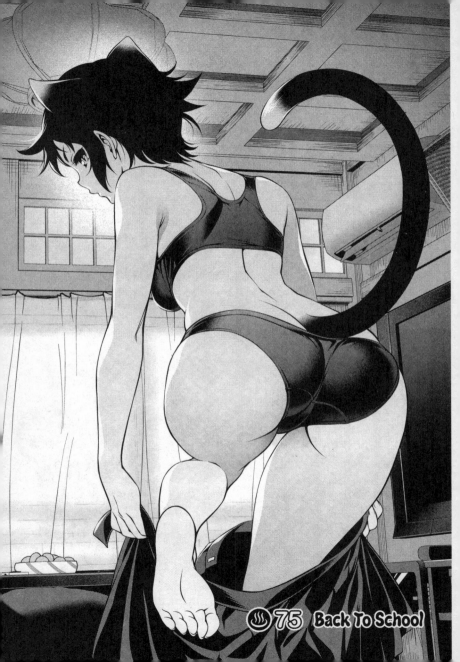

75 Back To School

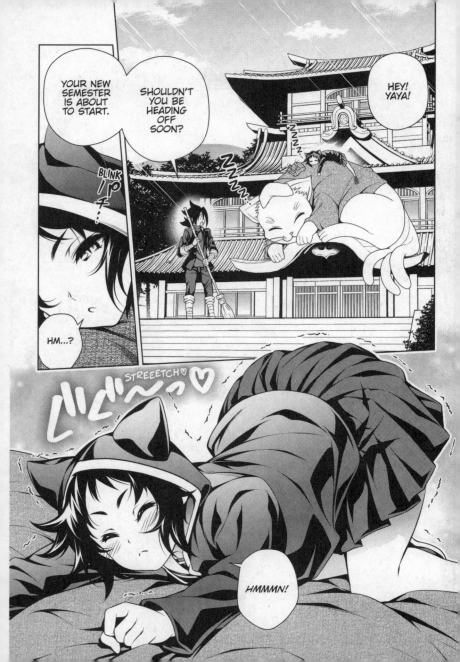

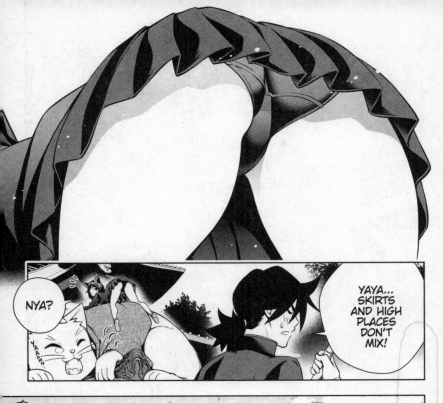

NYA?

YAYA... SKIRTS AND HIGH PLACES DON'T MIX!

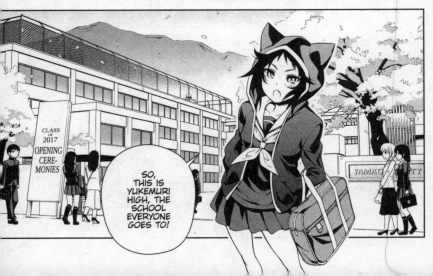

CLASS OF 2017 OPENING CERE- MONIES

SO, THIS IS YUKEMURI HIGH, THE SCHOOL EVERYONE GOES TO!

YAMAG-

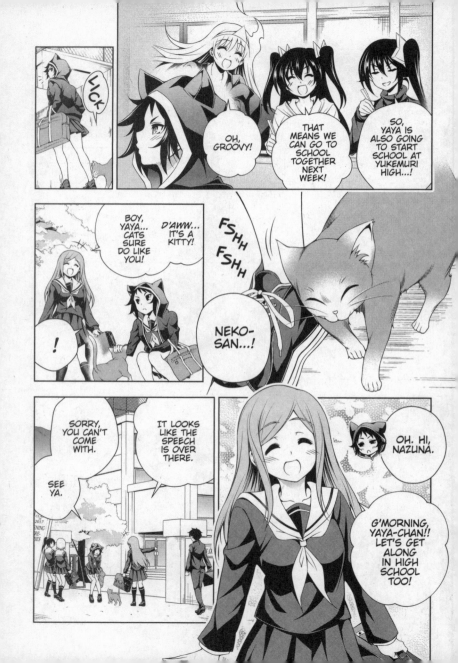

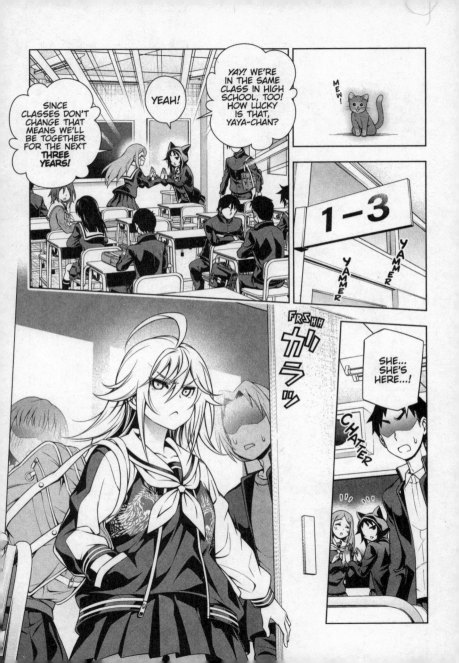

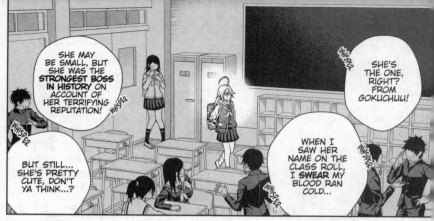

SHE MAY BE SMALL, BUT SHE WAS THE **STRONGEST BOSS IN HISTORY** ON ACCOUNT OF HER TERRIFYING REPUTATION!

SHE'S THE ONE, RIGHT? FROM GOKUCHUU!

BUT STILL... SHE'S PRETTY CUTE, DON'T YA THINK...?

WHEN I SAW HER NAME ON THE CLASS ROLL, I **SWEAR** MY BLOOD RAN COLD...

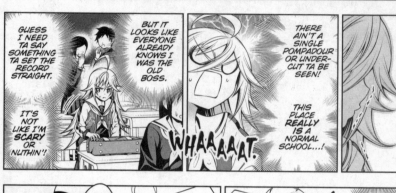

GUESS I NEED TA SAY SOMETHING TA SET THE RECORD STRAIGHT.

BUT IT LOOKS LIKE EVERYONE ALREADY KNOWS I WAS THE OLD BOSS.

IT'S NOT LIKE I'M **SCARY** OR NUTHIN'!

THERE AIN'T A SINGLE POMPADOUR OR UNDER-CUT TA BE SEEN!

THIS PLACE REALLY IS A NORMAL SCHOOL...!

WHAAAAAT.

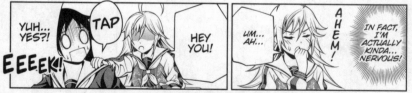

YUH... YES?!

TAP

HEY YOU!

EEEEK!

UM... AH...

A HEM!

IN FACT, I'M ACTUALLY KINDA... NERVOUS!

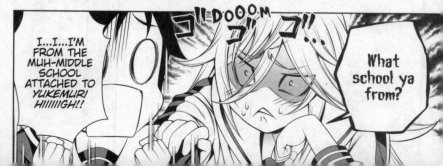

I...I...I'M FROM THE MUH-MIDDLE SCHOOL ATTACHED TO YUKEMURI HIIIIIIGH!!

ゴ "DOOOM" ゴゴ"

What school ya from?

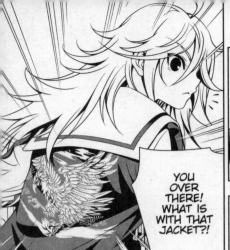

YOU OVER THERE! WHAT IS WITH THAT JACKET?!

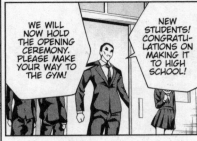

WE WILL NOW HOLD THE OPENING CEREMONY. PLEASE MAKE YOUR WAY TO THE GYM!

NEW STUDENTS! CONGRATU-LATIONS ON MAKING IT TO HIGH SCHOOL!

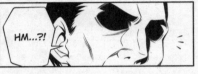

HM...?!

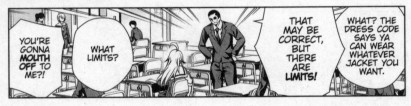

YOU'RE GONNA **MOUTH** OFF TO ME?!

WHAT LIMITS?

THAT MAY BE CORRECT, BUT THERE ARE **LIMITS!**

WHAT? THE DRESS CODE SAYS YA CAN WEAR WHATEVER JACKET YOU WANT.

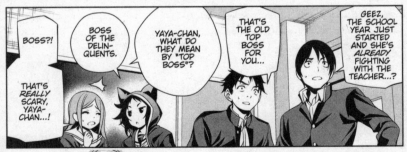

BOSS?!

BOSS OF THE DELIN-QUENTS.

YAYA-CHAN, WHAT DO THEY MEAN BY "TOP BOSS"?

THAT'S THE OLD TOP BOSS FOR YOU...

GEEZ, THE SCHOOL YEAR JUST STARTED AND SHE'S ALREADY FIGHTING WITH THE TEACHER...?

THAT'S REALLY SCARY, YAYA-CHAN...!

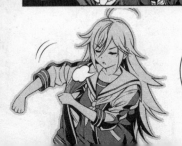

REALLY?

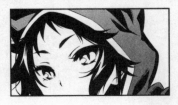

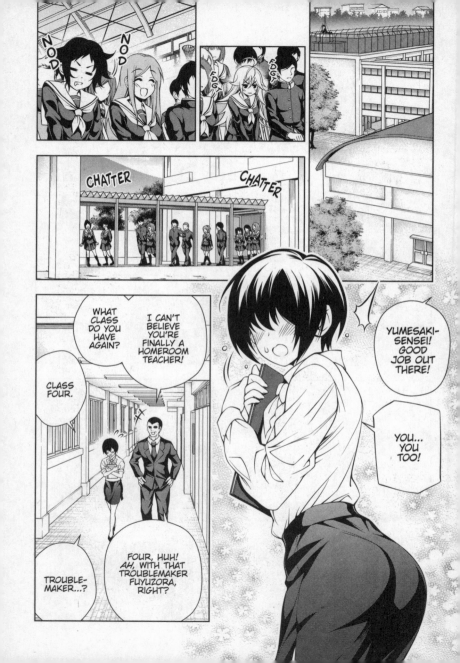

NOD NOD

FDGT FDGT

CHATTER   CHATTER

WHAT CLASS DO YOU HAVE AGAIN?

I CAN'T BELIEVE YOU'RE FINALLY A HOMEROOM TEACHER!

CLASS FOUR.

FOUR, HUH! AH, WITH THAT TROUBLEMAKER FUYUZORA, RIGHT?

TROUBLEMAKER...?

YUMESAKI-SENSEI! GOOD JOB OUT THERE!

YOU... YOU TOO!

DID... DID YOU SAY **A PSYCHIC**, SIR?

HE ALWAYS LEAVES THE ROOM A TOTAL MESS. I'VE NEVER SEEN HIM DO IT, BUT I KNOW IT'S HIM.

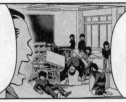

HE SAYS HE'S A **PSYCHIC** OR SOME NONSENSE. REAL STRANGE EGG, THAT ONE.

DON'T GET ME WRONG, HE'S AN EARNEST STUDENT AND ALL, BUT...

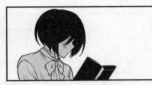

SOUNDS PRETTY ROUGH, SIR.

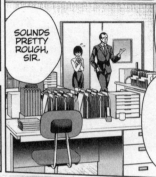

WE BARELY HAVE A SINGLE YEAR WITHOUT SOME INCIDENT THESE DAYS.

NOT TO MENTION THIS YEAR THERE'S THAT DELINQUENT FROM GOKUCHUU MIDDLE SCHOOL HERE AS WELL.

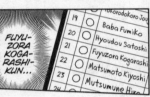

FUYU-ZORA KOGA-RASHI-KUN...

19	◯	Tokorodokoro Jou
20	◯	Baba Fumiko
21	◯	Hyoudou Satoshi
22	◯	Fuyuzora Kogarashi
23	◯	Matsumoto Kiyoshi
24		Mutsumune Hira

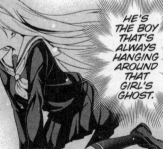

HE'S THE BOY THAT'S ALWAYS HANGING AROUND THAT GIRL'S GHOST.

THERE'S NO DOUBT ABOUT IT... HE'S THE REAL DEAL!

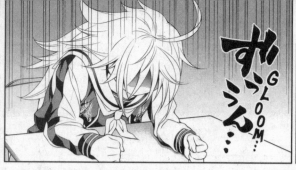

GLOOM...

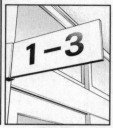

1-3

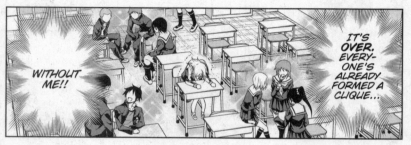

WITHOUT ME!!

IT'S OVER. EVERY-ONE'S ALREADY FORMED A CLIQUE...

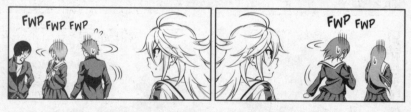

FWP FWP FWP

FWP FWP

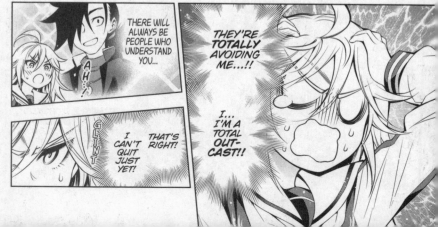

THERE WILL ALWAYS BE PEOPLE WHO UNDERSTAND YOU...

AH!?

THEY'RE TOTALLY AVOIDING ME...!!

I'M A TOTAL OUTCAST!!

GLINT

I CAN'T QUIT JUST YET!

THAT'S RIGHT!

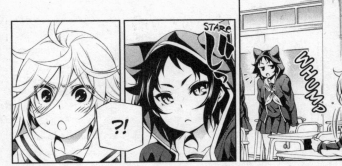

?!

STARE

THERE HAS TA BE SOME- ONE...

WHUMP

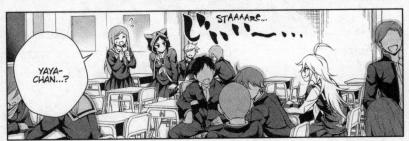

STAAAARE............

YAYA- CHAN...?

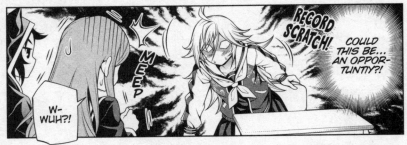

RECORD SCRATCH!

COULD THIS BE... AN OPPOR- TUNTIY?!

MEEP

W- WUH?!

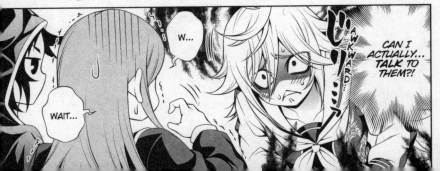

W...

CAN I ACTUALLY... TALK TO THEM?!

AWKWARD...

WAIT...

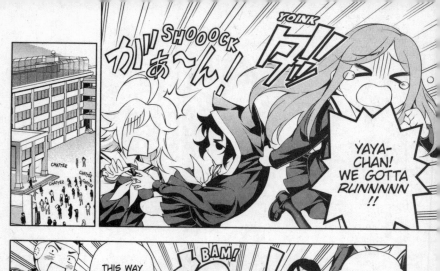

YAYA-CHAN! WE GOTTA RUNNNNN!!

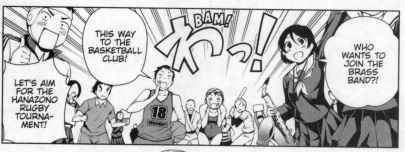

THIS WAY TO THE BASKETBALL CLUB!

LET'S AIM FOR THE HANAZONO RUGBY TOURNA-MENT!

WHO WANTS TO JOIN THE BRASS BAND?!

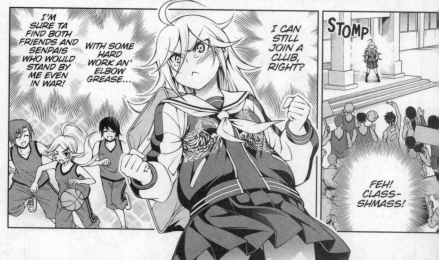

I'M SURE TA FIND BOTH FRIENDS AND SENPAIS WHO WOULD STAND BY ME EVEN IN WAR!

WITH SOME HARD WORK AN' ELBOW GREASE...

I CAN STILL JOIN A CLUB, RIGHT?

STOMP

FEH! CLASS-SHMASS!

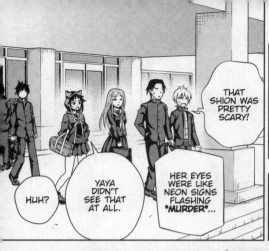

THAT SHION WAS PRETTY SCARY!

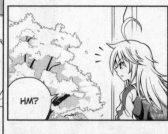

HM?

HUH?

YAYA DIDN'T SEE THAT AT ALL.

HER EYES WERE LIKE NEON SIGNS FLASHING *"MURDER"*...

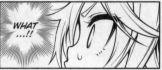

WHAT...!!

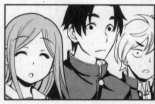

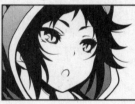

IT LOOKED TO ME LIKE SHE JUST WANTED TO TALK WITH US.

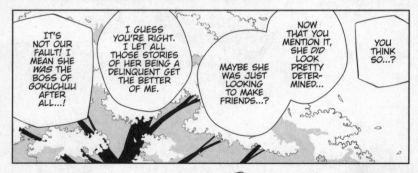

IT'S NOT OUR FAULT! I MEAN SHE WAS THE BOSS OF GOKUCHUU AFTER ALL....!

I GUESS YOU'RE RIGHT. I LET ALL THOSE STORIES OF HER BEING A DELINQUENT GET THE BETTER OF ME.

MAYBE SHE WAS JUST LOOKING TO MAKE FRIENDS...?

NOW THAT YOU MENTION IT, SHE *DID* LOOK PRETTY DETER-MINED...

YOU THINK SO...?

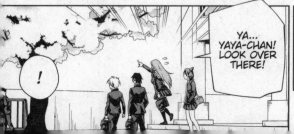

!

YA... YAYA-CHAN! LOOK OVER THERE!

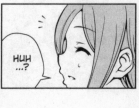

HUH ...?

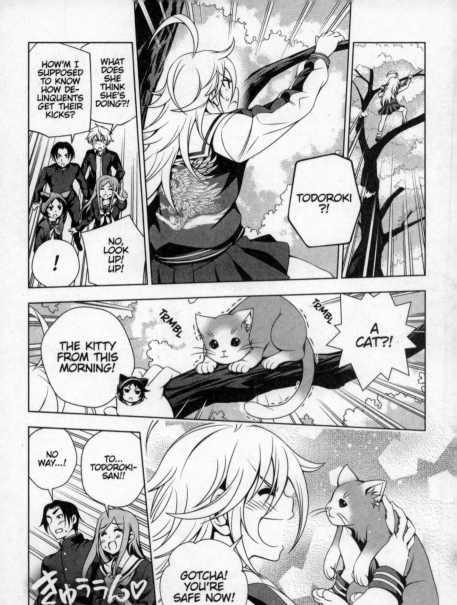

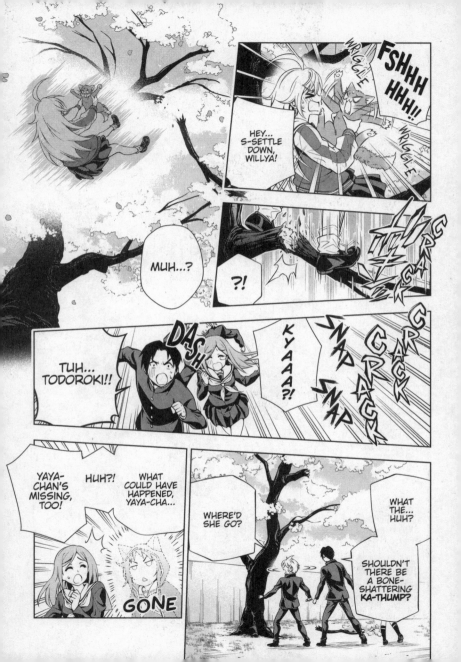

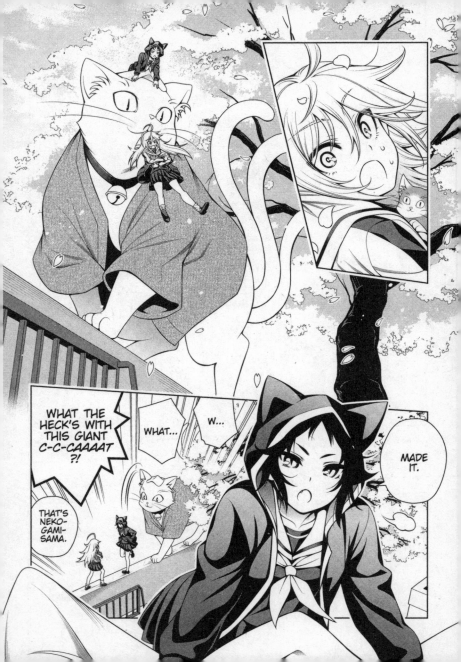

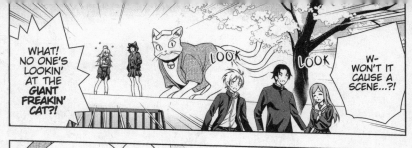

WHAT! NO ONE'S LOOKIN' AT THE GIANT FREAKIN' CAT?!

LOOK

LOOK

W-WON'T IT CAUSE A SCENE...?!

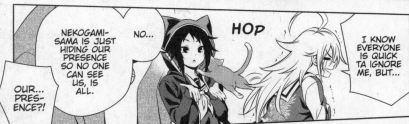

NEKOGAMI-SAMA IS JUST HIDING OUR PRESENCE SO NO ONE CAN SEE US, IS ALL.

NO...

HOP

OUR... PRESENCE?!

I KNOW EVERYONE IS QUICK TA IGNORE ME, BUT...

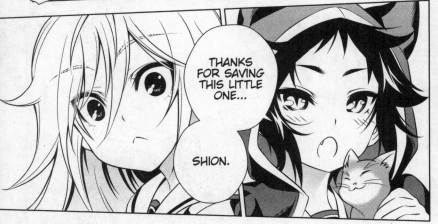

THANKS FOR SAVING THIS LITTLE ONE...

SHION.

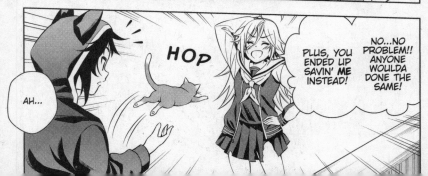

HOP

AH...

PLUS, YOU ENDED UP SAVIN' ME INSTEAD!

NO...NO PROBLEM!! ANYONE WOULDA DONE THE SAME!

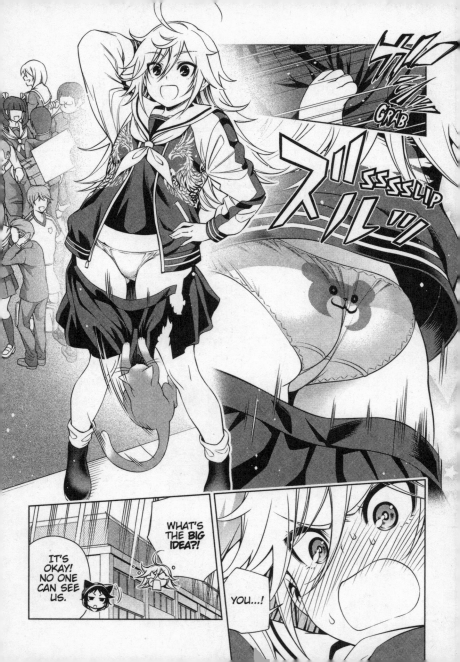

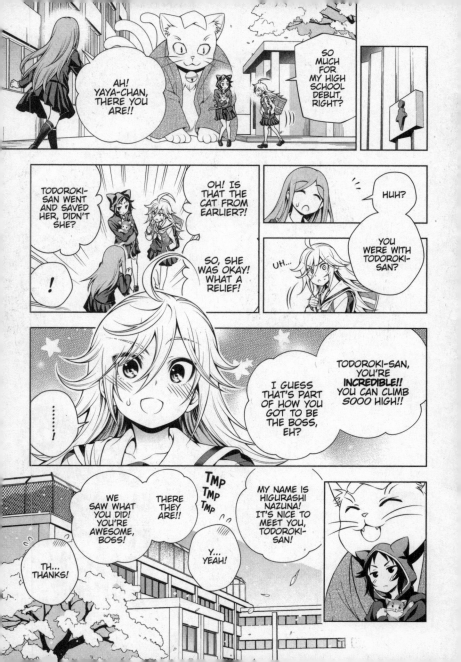

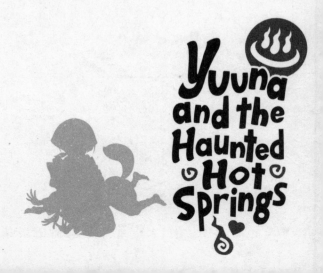

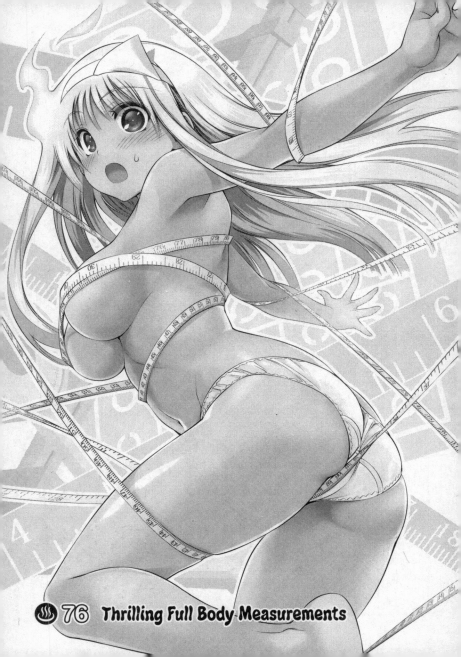

76 Thrilling Full Body Measurements

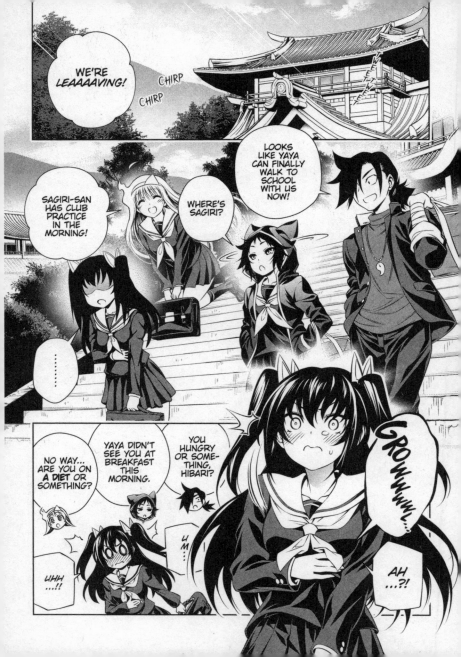

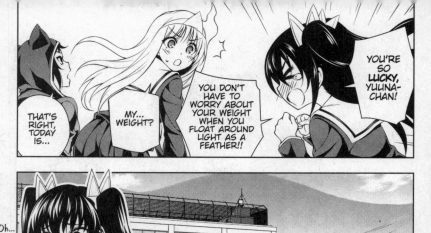

THAT'S RIGHT, TODAY IS...

MY... WEIGHT?

YOU DON'T HAVE TO WORRY ABOUT YOUR WEIGHT WHEN YOU FLOAT AROUND LIGHT AS A FEATHER!!

YOU'RE SO LUCKY, YUUNA-CHAN!

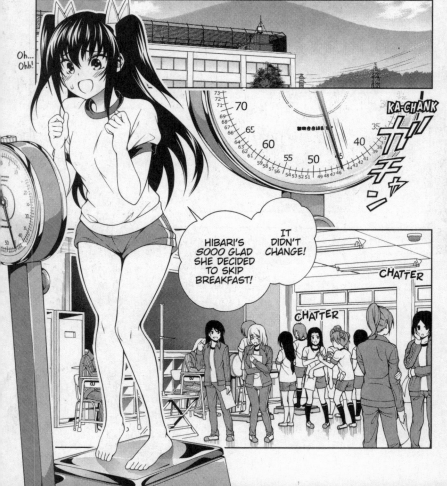

Oh... Ohh!

70

65

60

55   50

40

35

KA-CHANK

IT DIDN'T CHANGE!

HIBARI'S SOOO GLAD SHE DECIDED TO SKIP BREAKFAST!

CHATTER

CHATTER

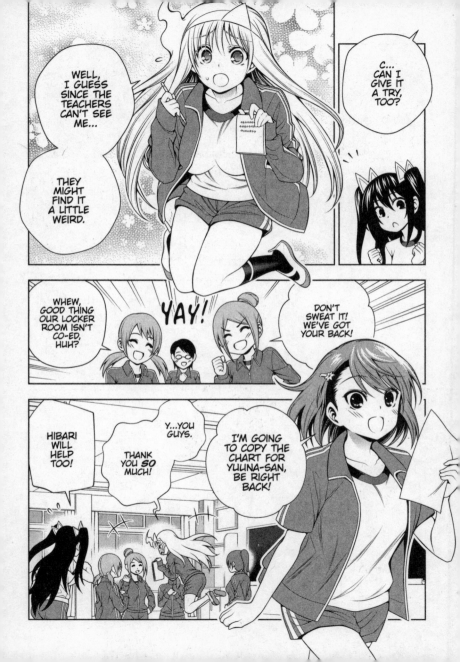

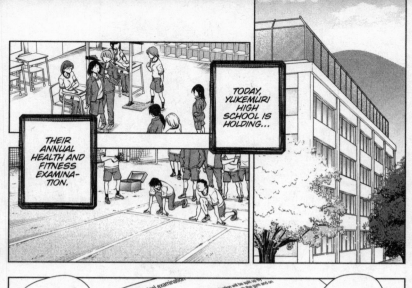

TODAY, YUKEMURI HIGH SCHOOL IS HOLDING...

THEIR ANNUAL HEALTH AND FITNESS EXAMINA-TION.

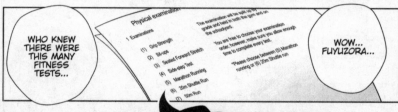

WHO KNEW THERE WERE THIS MANY FITNESS TESTS...

Physical examination

1. Examinations

(1) Grip Strength
(2) Sit-ups
(3) Seated Forward Stretch
(4) Side-step Test
(5) Marathon Running
(6) 20m Shuttle Run
(7) 50m Run

The examination will be split up by grade and held in both the gym and on the schoolyard.

You are free to choose your examination order, however, make sure you allow enough time to complete every test.

*Please choose between (5) Marathon running or (6) 20m Shuttle run

WOW... FUYUZORA...

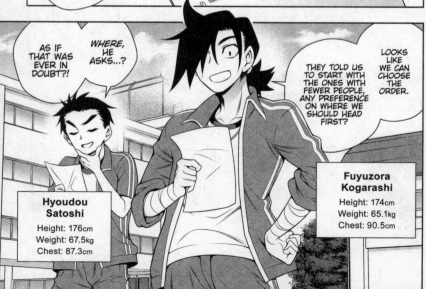

AS IF THAT WAS EVER IN DOUBT?!

WHERE, HE ASKS...?

THEY TOLD US TO START WITH THE ONES WITH FEWER PEOPLE, ANY PREFERENCE ON WHERE WE SHOULD HEAD FIRST?

LOOKS LIKE WE CAN CHOOSE THE ORDER.

Hyoudou Satoshi

Height: 176cm
Weight: 67.5kg
Chest: 87.3cm

Fuyuzora Kogarashi

Height: 174cm
Weight: 65.1kg
Chest: 90.5cm

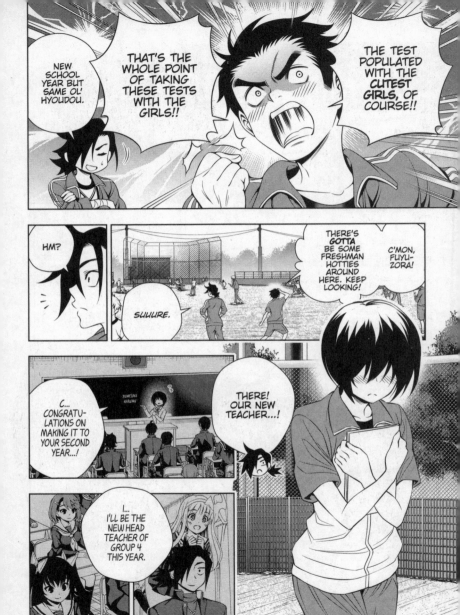

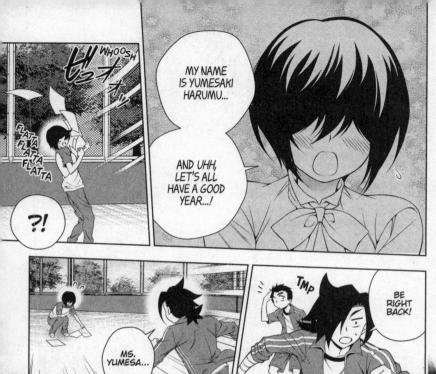

WHOOSH

FLATTA
FLATTA
FLATTA
FLATTA

?!

MY NAME IS YUMESAKI HARUMU...

AND UHH, LET'S ALL HAVE A GOOD YEAR...!

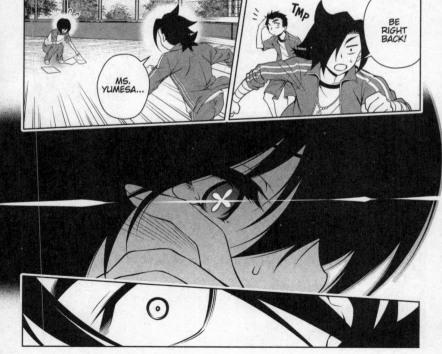

MS. YUMESA...

TMP

BE RIGHT BACK!

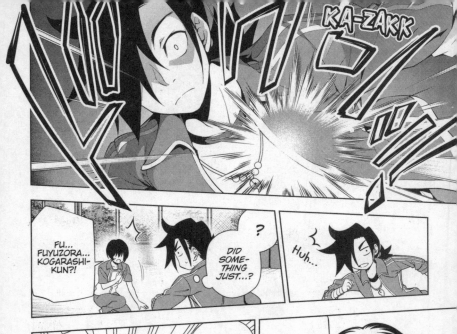
KA-ZAKK

FU... FUYUZORA... KOGARASHI-KUN?!

DID SOME-THING JUST...?

?

Huh...

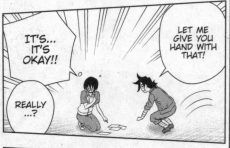

IT'S... IT'S OKAY!!

REALLY ...?

LET ME GIVE YOU HAND WITH THAT!

FUYUZORA-KUN... WHY ARE YOU...

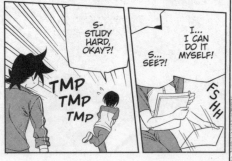

S-STUDY HARD, OKAY?!

S.... SEE?!

I... I CAN DO IT MYSELF!

TMP TMP TMP

FSHH

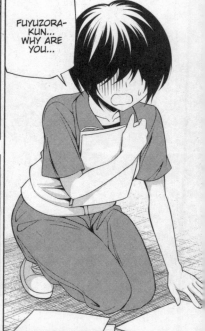

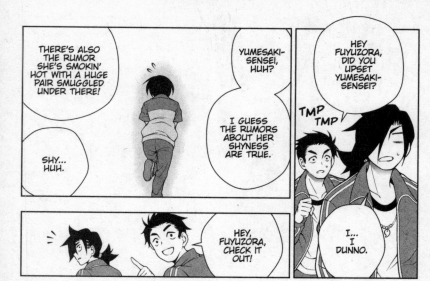

THERE'S ALSO THE RUMOR SHE'S SMOKIN' HOT WITH A HUGE PAIR SMUGGLED UNDER THERE!

YUMESAKI-SENSEI, HUH?

HEY FUYUZORA, DID YOU UPSET YUMESAKI-SENSEI?

I GUESS THE RUMORS ABOUT HER SHYNESS ARE TRUE.

SHY... HUH.

TMP TMP

I... I DUNNO.

HEY, FUYUZORA, CHECK IT OUT!

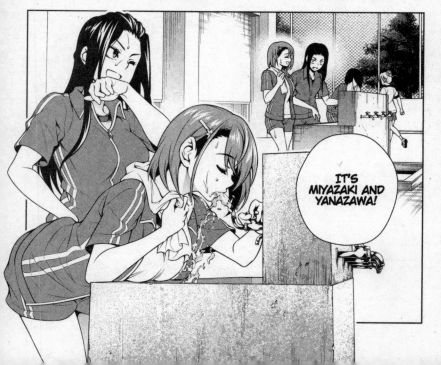

IT'S MIYAZAKI AND YANAZAWA!

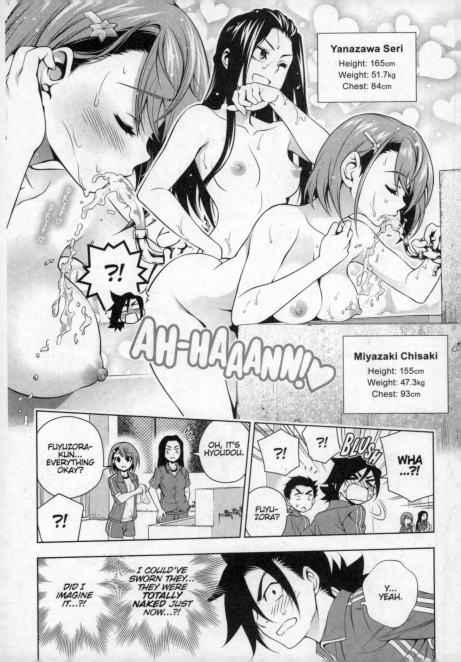

Yanazawa Seri
Height: 165cm
Weight: 51.7kg
Chest: 84cm

Miyazaki Chisaki
Height: 155cm
Weight: 47.3kg
Chest: 93cm

?!

AH-HAAANN!

FUYUZORA-KUN... EVERYTHING OKAY?

?!

OH, IT'S HYOUDOU.

?! ?!

BLUSH

WHA...?!

FUYU-ZORA?

DID I IMAGINE IT...?!

I COULD'VE SWORN THEY... THEY WERE TOTALLY NAKED JUST NOW...?!

Y... YEAH.

THE OTHER CLASSES SEEM TO THINK IT'S SOME KIND OF PRANK OR SOMETHING.

HUH...!

THAT'S RIGHT!

YUUNA'S DOING THE FITNESS EXAM!

WOOHOO!

JUST A LITTLE MORE! YOU CAN DO IT!

!

GOOD LUCK, YUUNA-CHAN!

HNN...

OOF...!

SQUIIISH

Yunohana Yuuna
Height: 153cm
Weight: 46.7kg
Chest: 93cm

HAAH... THAT'S AS FAR I CAN GO...!

YUUNA?!

STREEETCH

NOW OF ALL TIMES?!

WHAT'S GOING ON... SOME KIND OF YOKAI ATTACK?!

FU... FUYUZORA... YOU!

UHH.

CAN YOU GUIDE ME TO SAGIRI AND THE OTHERS...?!

HYOU... HYOUDOU! I CAN'T OPEN MY EYES RIGHT NOW...

WILL YOU JUST TAKE ME TO MY FRIENDS ALREADY?!

C'MOOOOON I WANNA SEE IT TOOO!!

YOU **ARE**, AREN'T YOU?!!

ARE YOU SEEING **PERVY THINGS** AGAIN...?!

IT'S BEEN AWHILE SINCE WE'VE COMPETED IN FITNESS TESTS LIKE THESE...

HIBARI.

NOT SINCE OUR FIRST YEAR OF MIDDLE SCHOOL... SAGIRI-CHAN.

JUST LET ME KNOW WHEN THEY'RE DONE...!

RIGHT... SO THEY **ARE** WEARING GYM CLOTHES... GOOD TO KNOW.

HIBARI-CHAN'S NOT SO BAD HERSELF.

EVEN WITH HER GYM CLOTHES SHE'S SO... **SHAPELY...**

THE AMENOS ARE **INCREDIBLE!**

FDGT

GULP...

FDGT

I SWEAR YOU ARE UNBELIEVABLE...!

BUT SINCE YOU SEEM TO BE THE ONLY ONE AFFECTED IT'S PROBABLY A BLESSING IN DISGUISE.

DID... YOU SEE **US** NAKED, TOO?!

B-BRIEFLY! I'M SORRY!

GIRLS LOOK **NAKED** TO YOU?!

NOW, IF I HAD TO WAGER A GUESS...

SOUNDS TO ME LIKE YOU'RE UNDER THE SPELL OF A SUCCUBUS.

SUCCUBUS... AH, LIKE YUMESAKI-SENSEI!

YUMESAKI-SENSEI?!

THEY TAKE CONTROL OF PEOPLE'S LUST AND MAKE THEM SEE ILLUSIONS!

A DEMON THAT SHOWS YOU *"NICE DREAMS,"* IF YA CATCH MY DRIFT?

SUCCU-BUS?

SO, YOU REALLY ARE A...

Y-YES!

I...I'M SORRY!!

I DIDN'T MEAN TO DO THAT TO YOU...!

Library

TO WEAR MY MAGIC-SEALING CONTACTS! BUT...

B-BUT THAT'S WHY I MADE SURE TODAY...

AS SUCH, MY CURSED EYE CAUSES PEOPLE TO SEE THINGS MOST OBSCENE!

SOMETHING FLEW INTO MY EYE WHEN I TRIPPED! I HAD TO TAKE THEM OUT! BUT ONLY FOR A MINUTE!

HEY, DON'T SWEAT IT!

WE KNOW YA DIDN'T MEAN TO, SENSEI.

I... YUMESAKI HARUMU...

INHERITED SUCCUBUS BLOOD. I'M REALLY ONLY A HALF-BREED.

YOU CAN HARDLY BE BLAMED FOR THIS FOOL'S TERRIBLE TIMING.

DOOOOM

BUT I HAD NO IDEA THAT SOMEONE WOULD MAKE EYE CONTACT WITH ME IN THAT BRIEF INSTANT...!

I QUICKLY PUT MY REPLACE-MENT LENS BACK ON!

WHEN SOMETHING LIKE THIS COMES UP THOUGH, WE DON'T HAVE MUCH CHOICE.

WE TAKE THEIR PRIVACY VERY SERIOUSLY AND HAVE A NO-INTERVENTION POLICY.

THE DEMON SLAYER NINJA FORCE KEEPS A CLOSE EYE ON ALL DEMONS AND HALF-BREEDS LIVING IN HUMAN SOCIETY.

SO, I TAKE IT YOU ALL KNEW ABOUT YUMESAKI-SENSEI?

WAIT... **WHAT?!**

I.... I CAN'T!

UM... ABOUT THAT.

BEFORE WE GO ON, PLEASE TURN KOGARASHI-KUN BACK TO NORMAL!

I CAN EVEN ORDER MY MAGIC-SEALING CONTACTS ONLINE! I CAN'T TELL YOU HOW CONVENIENT THAT IS...!

THAT'S WHY I'M SO THANKFUL FOR THE DEMON SLAYER NINJA FORCE!

ALL I CAN DO IS BE CAREFUL THAT STUFF LIKE THIS DOESN'T HAPPEN!

THING IS... I'M NOT VERY GOOD AT CONTROLLING MY SUCCUBUS POWERS!

THANKS FOR SHOPPING WITH US!

DEMON SLAYER MART

Weapons | Books | Scrolls | Miscellaneous | Even | Action
Electric Products | Food Hubs | Clothes

Real Body Contacts

TRUTH IS, I... I'M NOT SURE IF I CAN RELEASE YOU FROM THE CURSE!

I *REALLY* TRIED TO BE EXTRA CAREFUL AROUND FUYUZORA-KUN...!

WHILE OTHERS ARE MORE SUSCEP-TIBLE TO THEM!

PSYCHICS, LIKE THE DEMON SLAYER NINJA FORCE, ARE **USUALLY** HIGHLY RESISTANT TO CURSES!

THAT'S WHY YOU SHOULD ASK THE DEMON SLAYER--

THERE'S A CHANCE IT COULD GET **EVEN WORSE** THAN IT IS NOW...!

SO, **THAT'S** WHY YOU WERE AVOIDING ME.

WHAT A DIFFICULT LIFE...

DESPITE ALL HIS VAUNTED STRENGTH...!

NOT TO MENTION FUYUZORA-KUN IS CRAZY WEAK AGAINST MAGIC AND CURSES.

S... SORRY.

NO WAY...!

IF I MAY BUTT IN, SUCCUBUS CURSES ARE PARTICULARLY STRONG.

ATTEMPTING TO REMOVE IT COULD TAKE **DAYS**.

......!

BUT THAT'S A LITTLE DIFFERENT FROM REMOVING A CURSE ON MY OWN EYEBALLS!!

I COMPENSATED BY TRAINING MYSELF TO FEND OFF SPIRITS...

MY POWERS AS A PSYCHIC CAUSE ME TO BE MORE VULNERABLE TO SPIRITUAL ENERGY.

HE'S PROBABLY HAD TO GO THROUGH QUITE A LOT.

I SEE...

FUYUZORA-KUN ALSO HAS HIS OWN PROBLEMS.

!

FLASH

I... I UNDERSTAND!

CLENCH

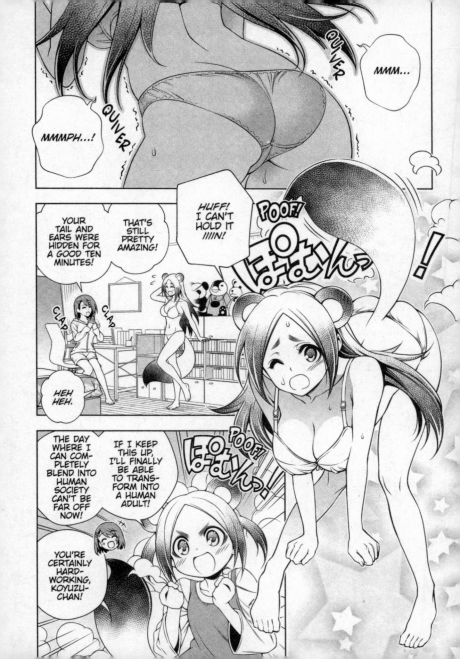

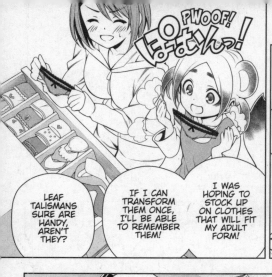
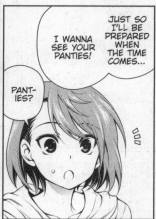
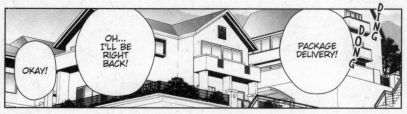
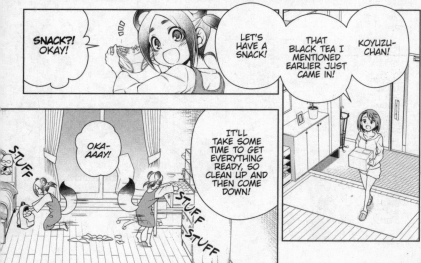

YAAAAY! ALL DONE~!

TMP TMP

THE NEXT DAY.

WHY, GOOD MORNING FUYUZORA-KUN! YUUNA-SAN!

CHISAKI-SAN! GOOD MORNING!!

MORNING MIYAZAKI!

YOU TWO ARE HERE EARLY TODAY.

I'M ON CLASS DUTY TODAY!

FWIP♥

WHOOOSH

?!

BIT BREEZY TODAY, HUH?

CLAK

S... SORRY!

SMAP

MEEP ...!

!

POOF!

SURE!

I GUESS WE SHOULD GET BACK TO OUR SEATS.

BING BONG
BING BONG

WHAT WAS THAT...?

FWISH...

PAT PAT

TOUCH

TH-THIS FEELING...

COULD IT BE...?!

WHAT CAN I DO?!

WH... WHAT SHOULD I DO...

HM?

YESTER-DAY, DID I...

ACCIDENTALLY MIX UP REAL PANTIES FOR ONE OF MY LEAF TALISMAN PANTIES AND TAKE THEM HOME WITH ME...?!

THIS IS THE ONLY ONE THAT WON'T TURN BACK INTO A TALISMAN.

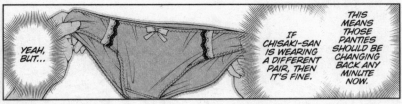

YEAH, BUT...

IF CHISAKI-SAN IS WEARING A DIFFERENT PAIR, THEN IT'S FINE.

THIS MEANS THOSE PANTIES SHOULD BE CHANGING BACK ANY MINUTE NOW.

N... NAKAI-SAN! CAN I USE YOUR PHONE REAL QUICK?!

OF COURSE!

IF SHE IS WEARING THAT PARTICULAR PAIR TO SCHOOL...

GASP

KOYUZU-CHAAAAN!!

OKAY... LET'S SEE.

MIYAZAKI!

YUH... YES?!

HMMMN... I CAN'T FOCUS ON THE LESSON LIKE THIS...!

WRIGGLE

WRIGGLE

DUN-DUNNN!

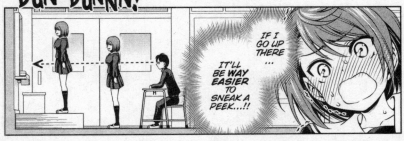

IF I GO UP THERE...

IT'LL BE WAY EASIER TO SNEAK A PEEK...!!

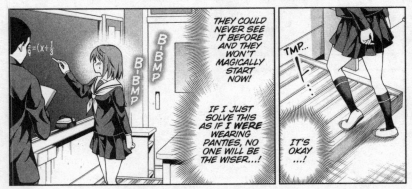

$\frac{x}{6} \div (x + \frac{1}{3})$

B-BMP

B-BMP

THEY COULD NEVER SEE IT BEFORE AND THEY WON'T MAGICALLY START NOW!

IF I JUST SOLVE THIS AS IF I WERE WEARING PANTIES, NO ONE WILL BE THE WISER...!

TMP...

...

IT'S OKAY...!

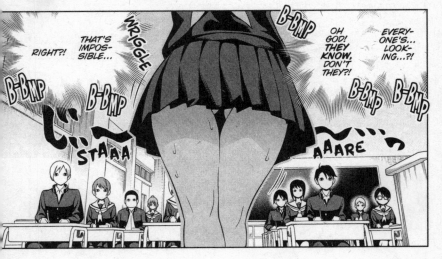

RIGHT?!

THAT'S IMPOSSIBLE...

WRIGGLE

B-BMP

OH GOD! THEY KNOW, DON'T THEY?!

EVERY- ONE'S... LOOK- ING...?!

B-BMP

B-BMP

B-BMP

B-BMP

STAAA

AAARE

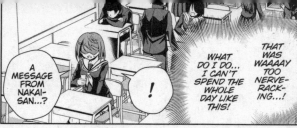

A MESSAGE FROM NAKAI-SAN...?

!

WHAT DO I DO... I CAN'T SPEND THE WHOLE DAY LIKE THIS!

THAT WAS WAAAAY TOO NERVE-RACK-ING...!

BING BONG...

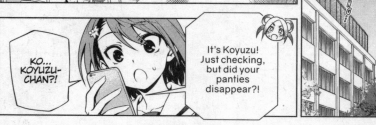

KO... KOYUZU-CHAN?!

It's Koyuzu! Just checking, but did your panties disappear?!

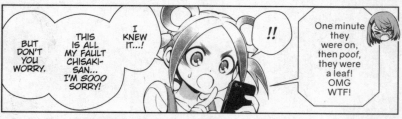

BUT DON'T YOU WORRY.

THIS IS ALL MY FAULT CHISAKI-SAN... I'M SOOO SORRY!

I KNEW IT...!

!!

One minute they were on, then poof, they were a leaf! OMG WTF!

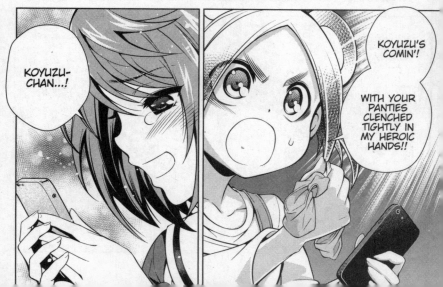

KOYUZU-CHAN...!

KOYUZU'S COMIN'!

WITH YOUR PANTIES CLENCHED TIGHTLY IN MY HEROIC HANDS!!

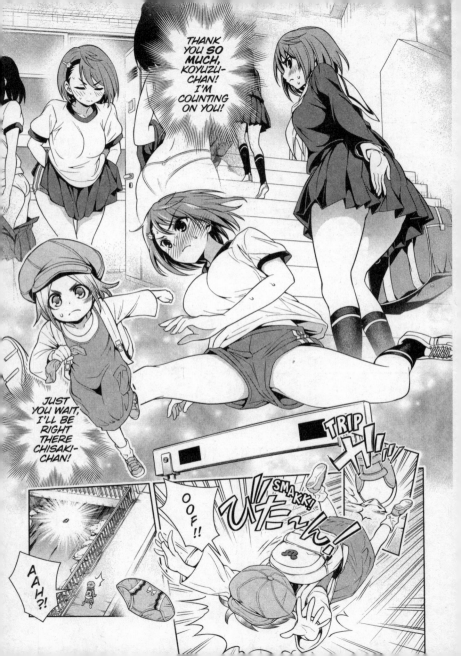

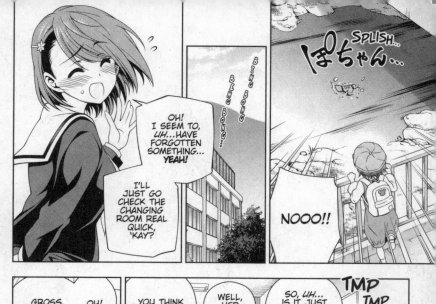

SPLISH...
ぽちゃん...

BING BONG...
BING BONG...

OH! I SEEM TO, *UH*...HAVE FORGOTTEN SOMETHING... YEAH!

I'LL JUST GO CHECK THE CHANGING ROOM REAL QUICK, 'KAY?

NOOO!!

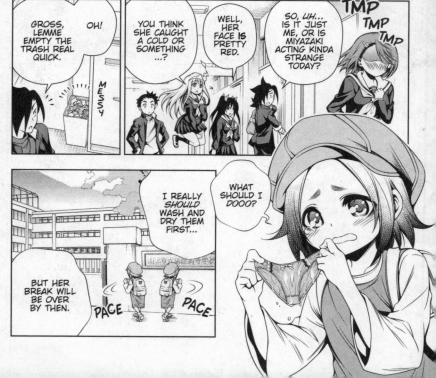

GROSS, LEMME EMPTY THE TRASH REAL QUICK.

OH!

MESSY

YOU THINK SHE CAUGHT A COLD OR SOMETHING ...?

WELL, HER FACE **IS** PRETTY RED.

SO, *UH*... IS IT JUST ME, OR IS MIYAZAKI ACTING KINDA STRANGE TODAY?

TMP
TMP
TMP

I REALLY *SHOULD* WASH AND DRY THEM FIRST...

WHAT SHOULD I DOOO?

BUT HER BREAK WILL BE OVER BY THEN.

PACE

PACE

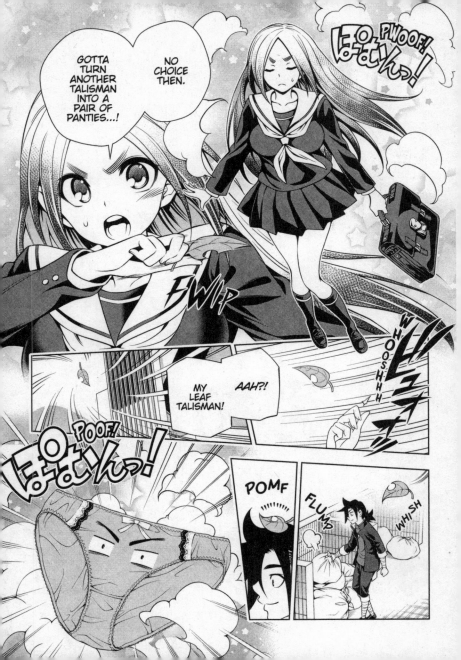

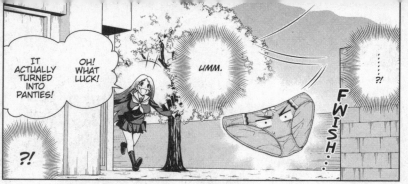

IT ACTUALLY TURNED INTO PANTIES!

OH! WHAT LUCK!

UMM.

......?!

?!

FWISH...

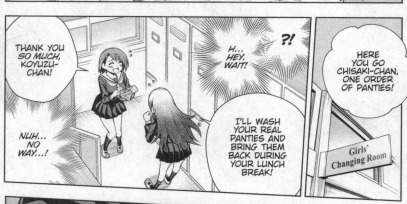

THANK YOU SO MUCH, KOYUZU-CHAN!

H... HEY. WAIT!

?!

HERE YOU GO CHISAKI-CHAN, ONE ORDER OF PANTIES!

NUH... NO WAY...!

I'LL WASH YOUR REAL PANTIES AND BRING THEM BACK DURING YOUR LUNCH BREAK!

Girls' Changing Room

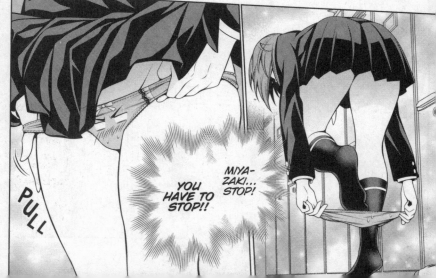

PULL

YOU HAVE TO STOP!!

MIYA-ZAKI... STOP!

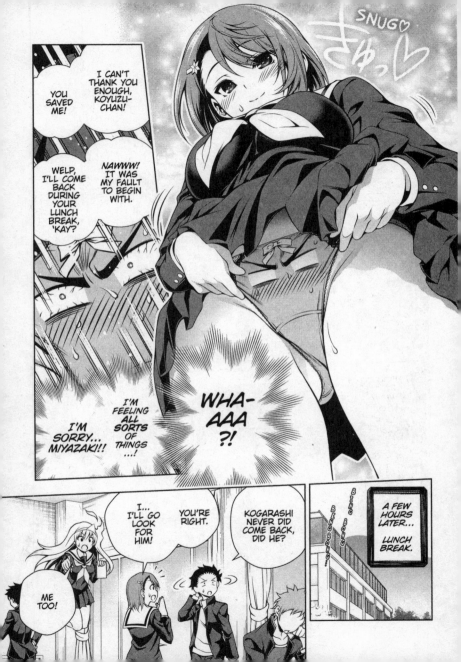

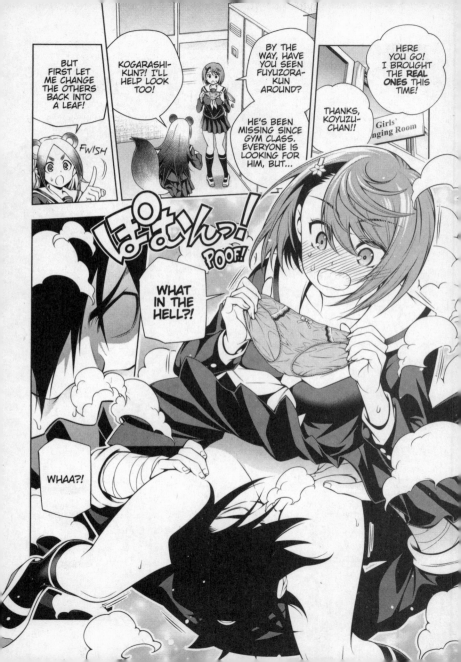

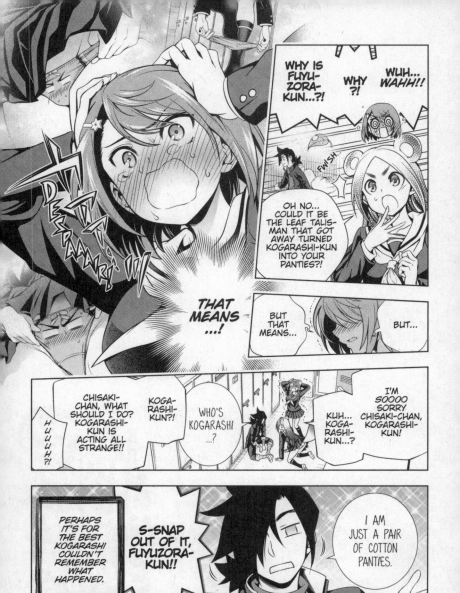

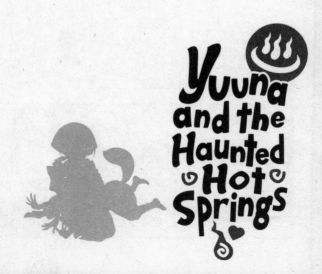

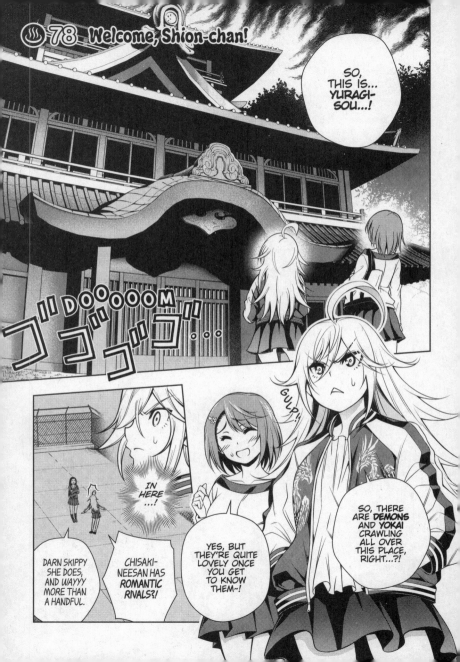

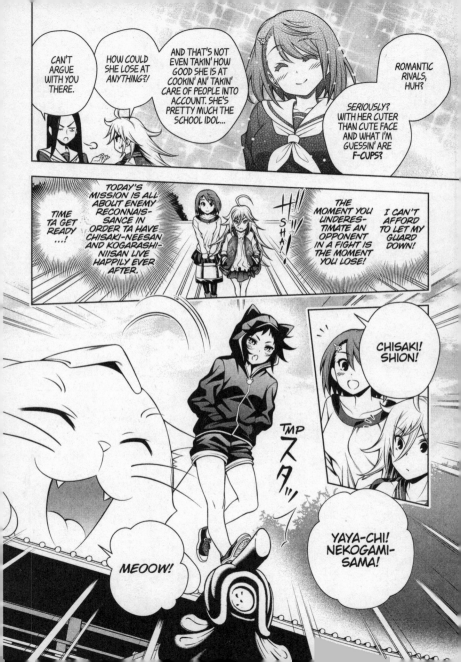

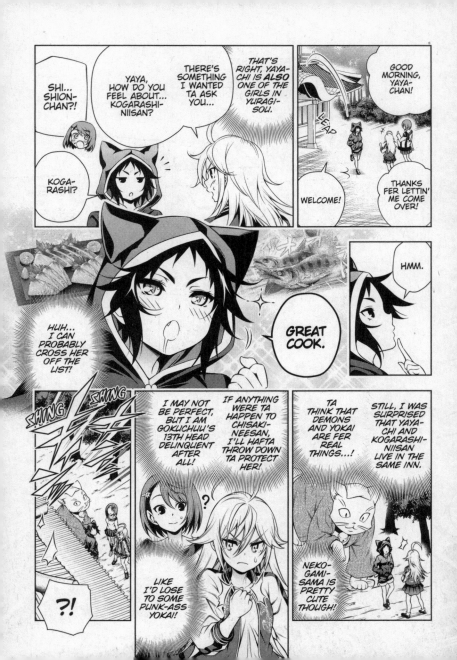

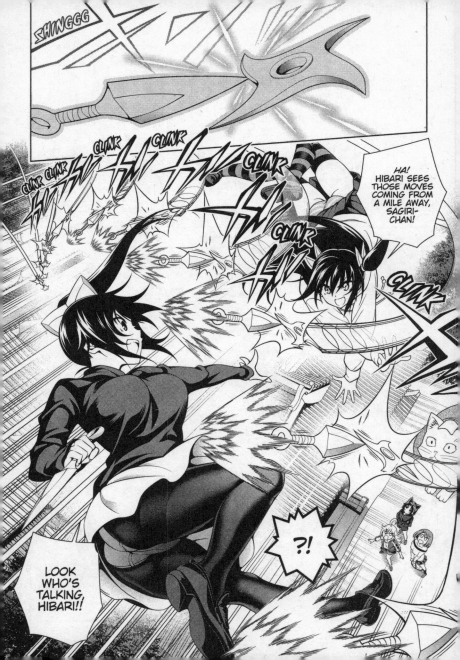

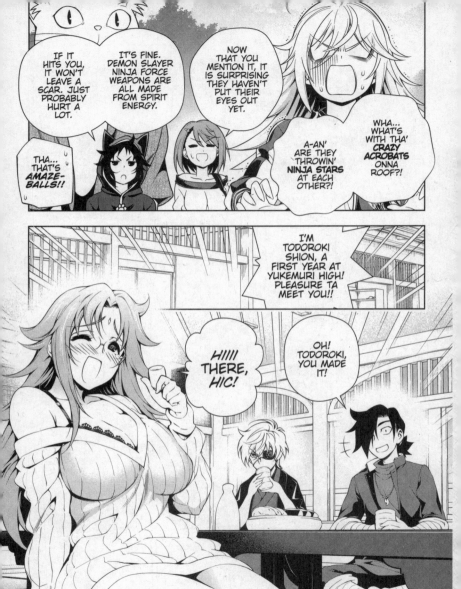

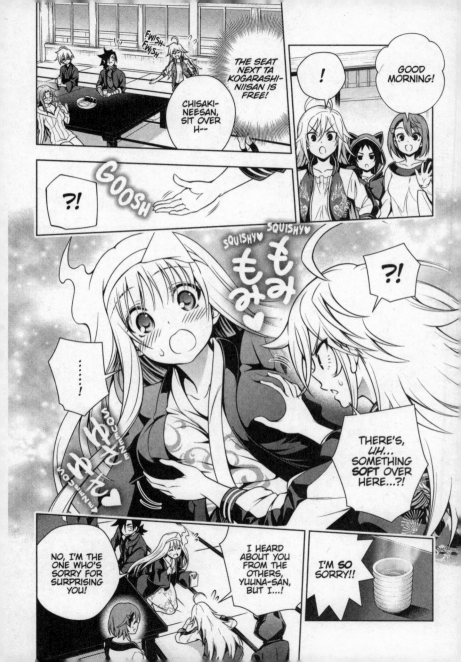

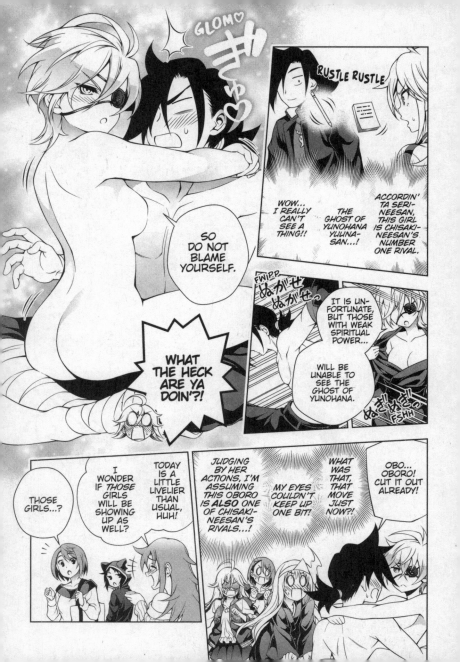

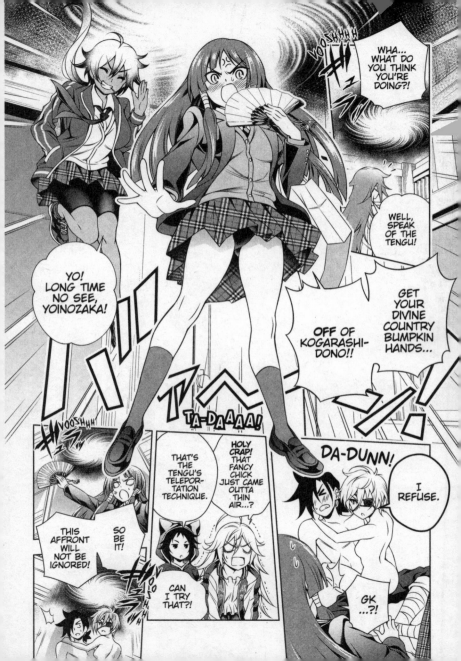

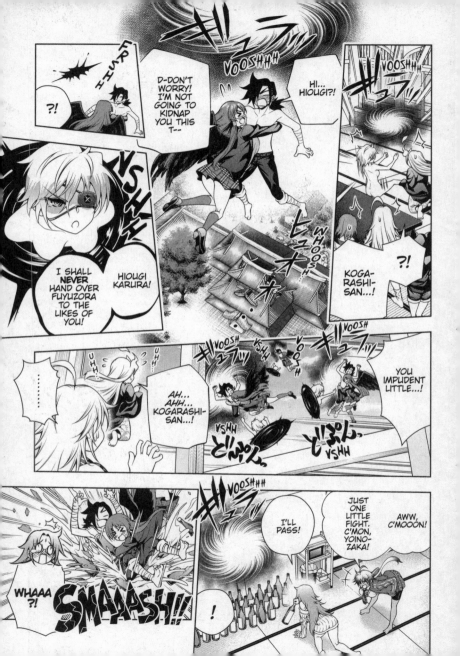

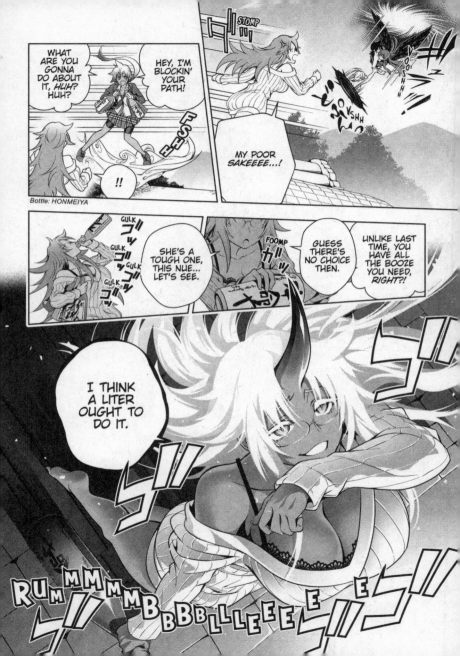

WHAT ARE YOU GONNA DO ABOUT IT, *HUH?* HUH?

HEY, I'M BLOCKIN' YOUR PATH!

STOMP

!!

Bottle: HONMEIYA

MY POOR SAKEEEE...!

GULK
GULK
GULK
GULK

SHE'S A TOUGH ONE, THIS NUE... LET'S SEE.

FOOMP

GUESS THERE'S NO CHOICE THEN.

UNLIKE LAST TIME, YOU HAVE ALL THE BOOZE YOU NEED, *RIGHT?!*

I THINK A LITER OUGHT TO DO IT.

RUMMMMMMBBBBLLLEEEEE

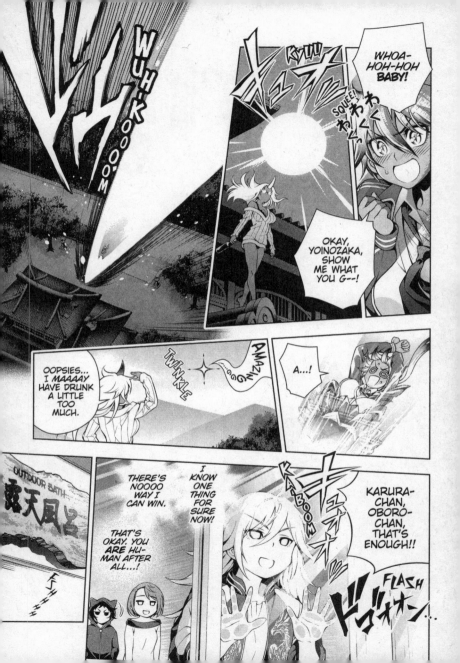

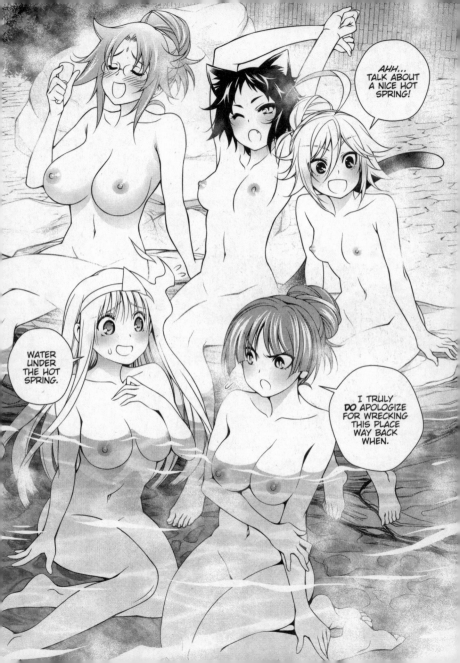

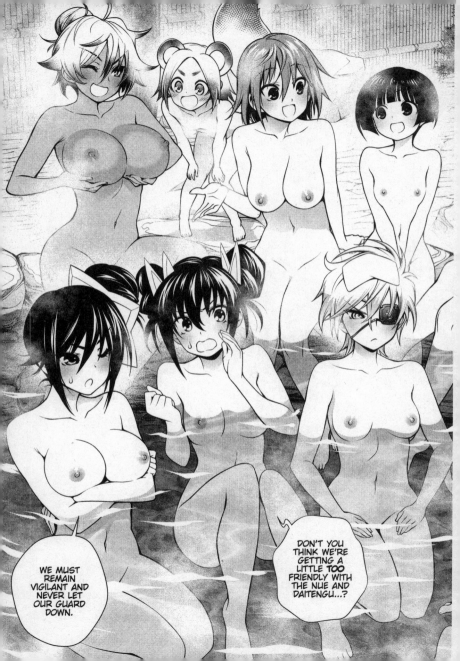

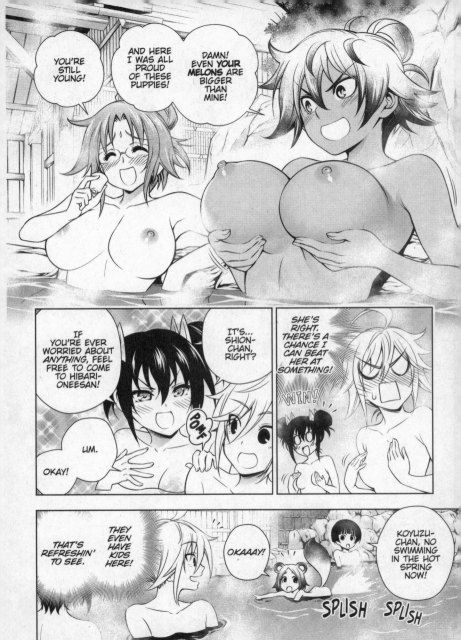

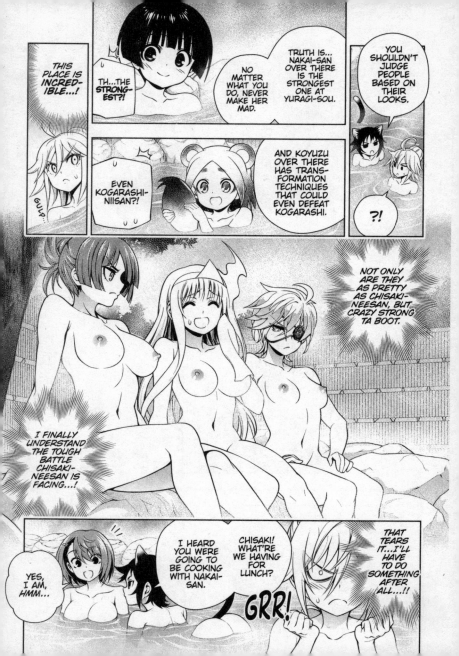

THIS PLACE IS INCREDIBLE...!

TH...THE STRONGEST?!

NO MATTER WHAT YOU DO, NEVER MAKE HER MAD.

TRUTH IS... NAKAI-SAN OVER THERE IS THE STRONGEST ONE AT YURAGI-SOU.

YOU SHOULDN'T JUDGE PEOPLE BASED ON THEIR LOOKS.

GULP...

EVEN KOGARASHI-NIISAN?!

AND KOYUZU OVER THERE HAS TRANS-FORMATION TECHNIQUES THAT COULD EVEN DEFEAT KOGARASHI.

?!

NOT ONLY ARE THEY AS PRETTY AS CHISAKI-NEESAN, BUT CRAZY STRONG TA BOOT.

I FINALLY UNDERSTAND THE TOUGH BATTLE CHISAKI-NEESAN IS FACING...!

YES, I AM, HMM...

I HEARD YOU WERE GOING TO BE COOKING WITH NAKAI-SAN.

CHISAKI! WHAT'RE WE HAVING FOR LUNCH?

THAT TEARS IT... I'LL HAVE TO DO SOMETHING AFTER ALL...!!

GRR!

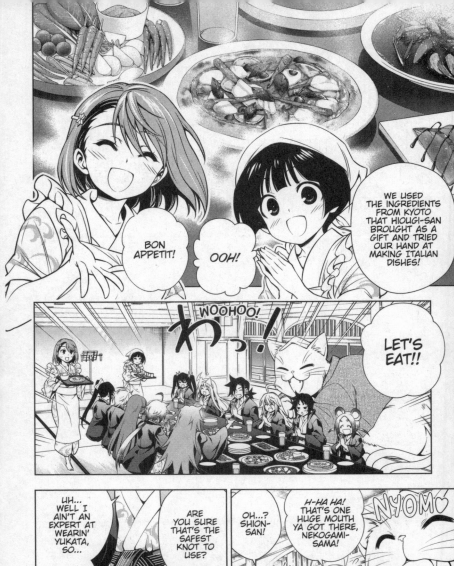

BON APPETIT!

OOH!

WE USED THE INGREDIENTS FROM KYOTO THAT HIOUGI-SAN BROUGHT AS A GIFT AND TRIED OUR HAND AT MAKING ITALIAN DISHES!

WOOHOO!

LET'S EAT!!

UH... WELL I AIN'T AN EXPERT AT WEARIN' YUKATA, SO...

AHH... I'M SURE IT'S FINE!

ARE YOU SURE THAT'S THE SAFEST KNOT TO USE?

OH...? SHION-SAN!

H-HA HA! THAT'S ONE HUGE MOUTH YA GOT THERE, NEKOGAMI-SAMA!

NYOM♡

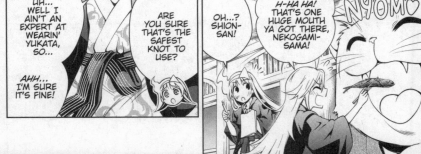

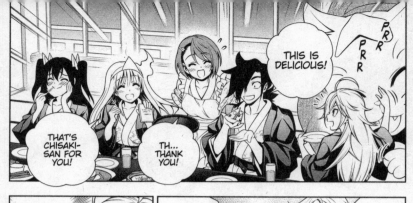

THIS IS DELICIOUS!

PRRR

THAT'S CHISAKI-SAN FOR YOU!

TH... THANK YOU!

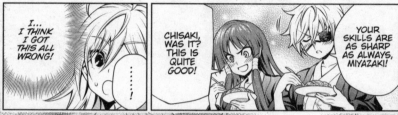

I... I THINK I GOT THIS ALL WRONG!

......!

CHISAKI, WAS IT? THIS IS QUITE GOOD!

YOUR SKILLS ARE AS SHARP AS ALWAYS, MIYAZAKI!

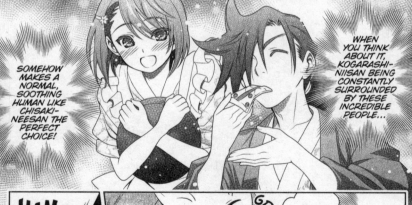

SOMEHOW MAKES A NORMAL, SOOTHING HUMAN LIKE CHISAKI-NEESAN THE PERFECT CHOICE!

WHEN YOU THINK ABOUT IT, KOGARASHI-NIISAN BEING CONSTANTLY SURROUNDED BY THESE INCREDIBLE PEOPLE...

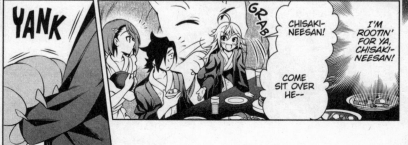

YANK

GRAB

CHISAKI-NEESAN!

COME SIT OVER HE--

I'M ROOTIN' FOR YA, CHISAKI-NEESAN!

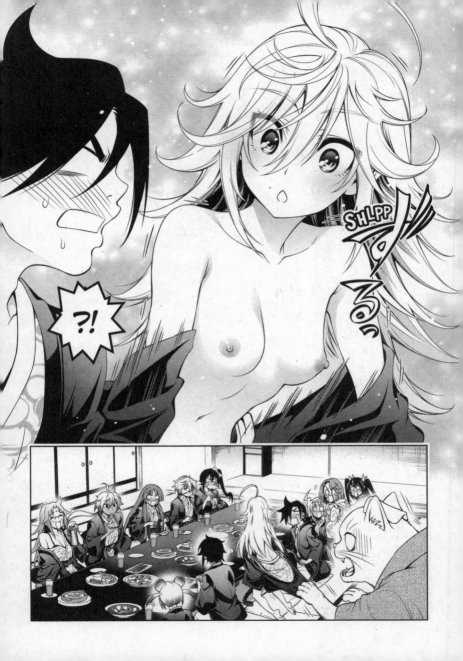

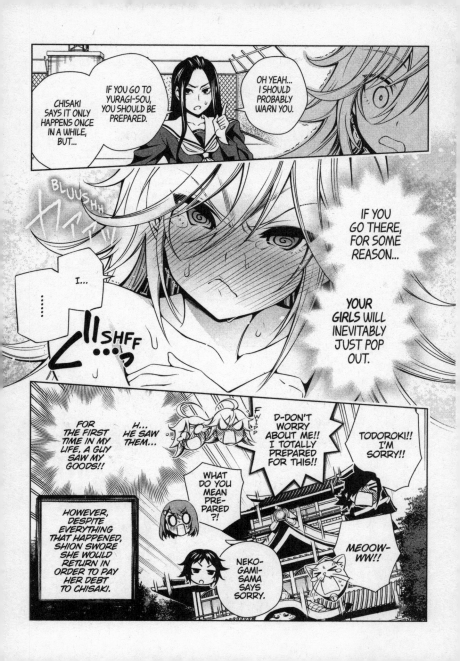

OH YEAH... I SHOULD PROBABLY WARN YOU.

IF YOU GO TO YURAGI-SOU, YOU SHOULD BE PREPARED.

CHISAKI SAYS IT ONLY HAPPENS ONCE IN A WHILE, BUT...

BLUUSHH

I...

......

SHFF

IF YOU GO THERE, FOR SOME REASON...

YOUR GIRLS WILL INEVITABLY JUST POP OUT.

FOR THE FIRST TIME IN MY LIFE, A GUY SAW MY GOODS!!

H... HE SAW THEM...

FWIP

D-DON'T WORRY ABOUT ME!! I TOTALLY PREPARED FOR THIS!!

TODOROKI!! I'M SORRY!!

WHAT DO YOU MEAN PRE- PARED?!

HOWEVER, DESPITE EVERYTHING THAT HAPPENED, SHION SWORE SHE WOULD RETURN IN ORDER TO PAY HER DEBT TO CHISAKI.

NEKO- GAMI- SAMA SAYS SORRY.

MEOOW- WW!!

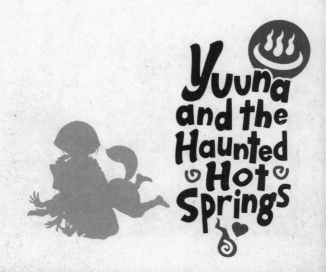

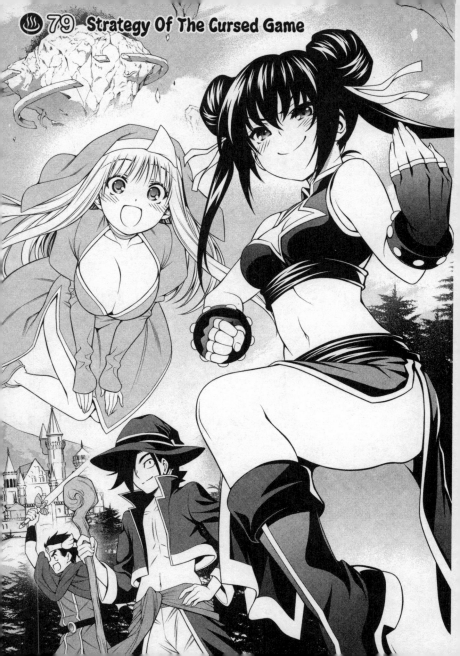

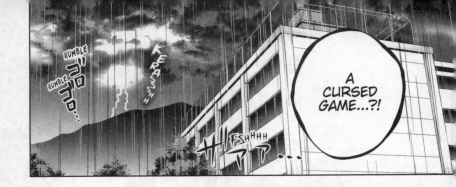

A CURSED GAME...?!

SO STRONG WAS HIS DYING DESIRE TO HAVE SOMEONE, ANYONE PLAY HIS GAME THAT HIS LINGERING EMOTION CURSED IT AS HE DIED.

BUT AFTER NEGLECTING HIS HEALTH TO MAKE DEADLINE, HE PASSED AWAY RIGHT BEFORE IT WAS RELEASED.

YEAH... IT'S SAID THAT THE GAME WAS CREATED BY AN INDIE GAME DEVELOPER...

THEY SAY ON LONELY NIGHTS WHEN BANDWITH SPEEDS ARE LOW, THE GAME WILL APPEAR ON INDIE GAME DOWNLOADING SITES...!

THOUGH THE GAME WAS NEVER RELEASED TO THE PUBLIC, **THE GAME ITSELF** DESIRES TO BE PLAYED.

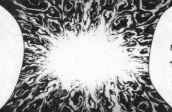

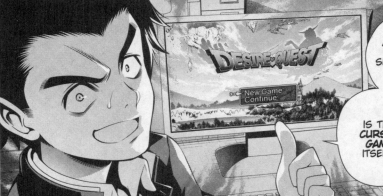

AND I'M PRETTY SURE THIS HERE...

IS THE **CURSED GAME** ITSELF!

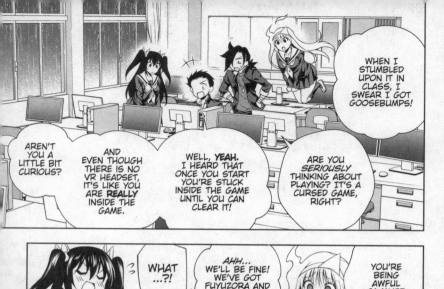

WHEN I STUMBLED UPON IT IN CLASS, I SWEAR I GOT GOOSEBUMPS!

AREN'T YOU A LITTLE BIT CURIOUS?

AND EVEN THOUGH THERE IS NO VR HEADSET, IT'S LIKE YOU ARE **REALLY** INSIDE THE GAME.

WELL, **YEAH.** I HEARD THAT ONCE YOU START YOU'RE STUCK INSIDE THE GAME UNTIL YOU CAN CLEAR IT!

ARE YOU *SERIOUSLY* THINKING ABOUT PLAYING? IT'S A CURSED GAME, RIGHT?

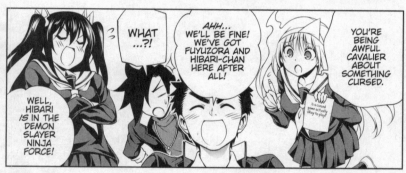

WHAT ...?!

AHH... WE'LL BE FINE! WE'VE GOT FUYUZORA AND HIBARI-CHAN HERE AFTER ALL!

YOU'RE BEING AWFUL CAVALIER ABOUT SOMETHING CURSED.

WELL, HIBARI *IS* IN THE DEMON SLAYER NINJA FORCE!

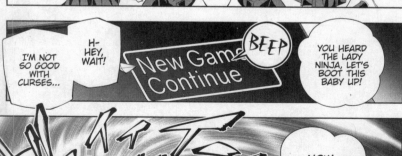

I'M NOT SO GOOD WITH CURSES...

H- HEY, WAIT!

New Game
Continue

BEEP

YOU HEARD THE LADY NINJA, LET'S BOOT THIS BABY UP!

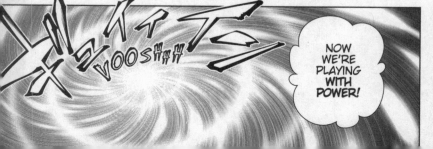

VOOSH!!!

NOW WE'RE PLAYING WITH POWER!

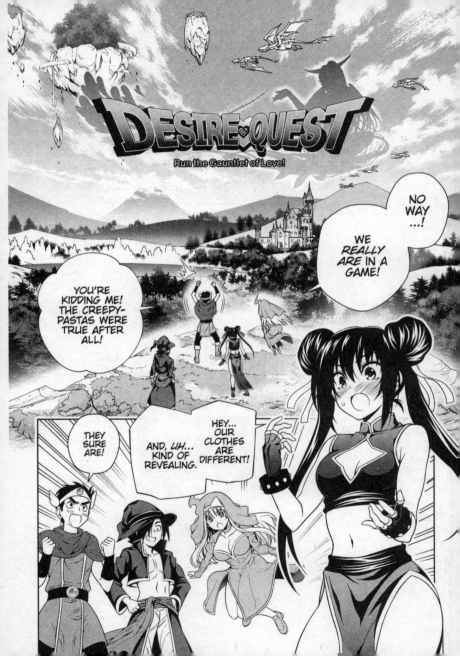

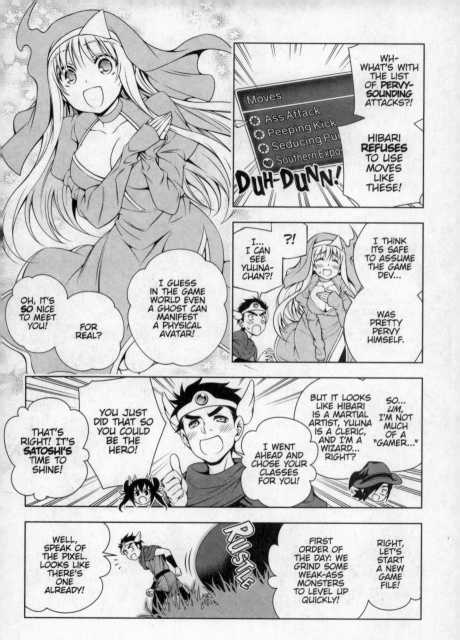

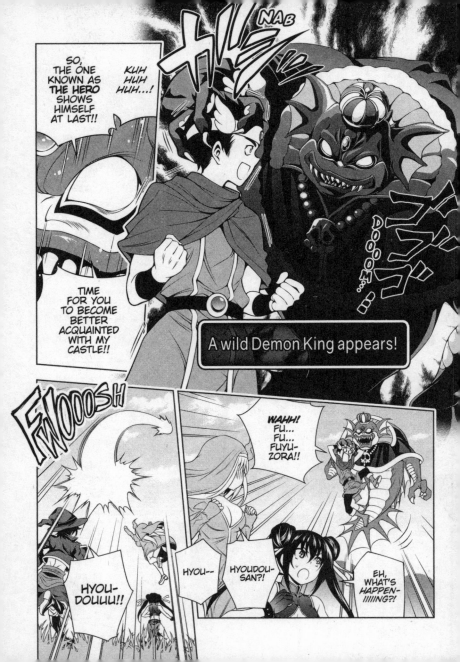

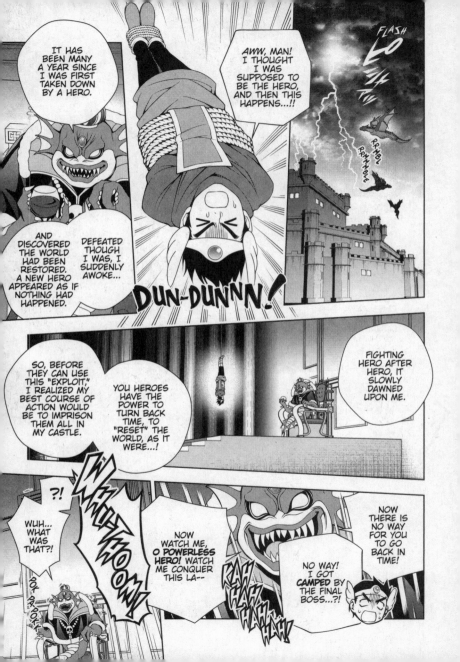

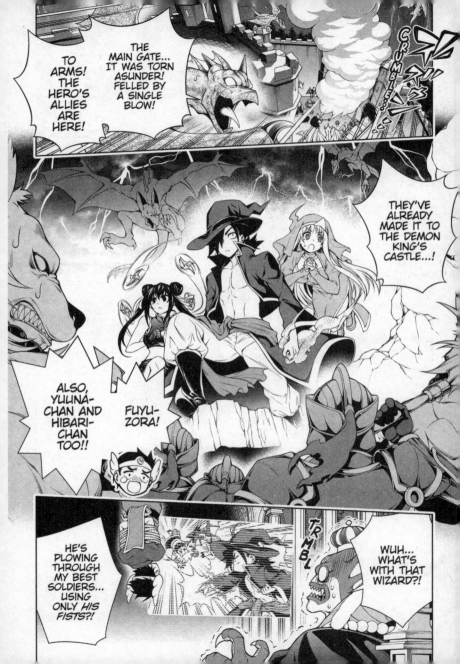

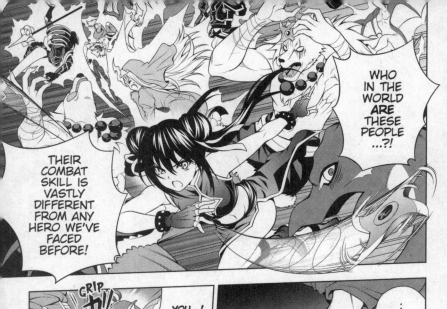
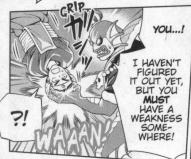
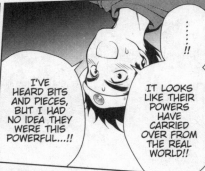
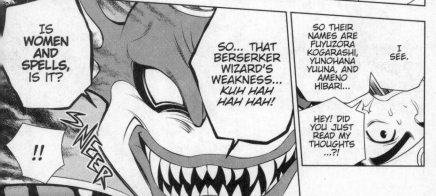

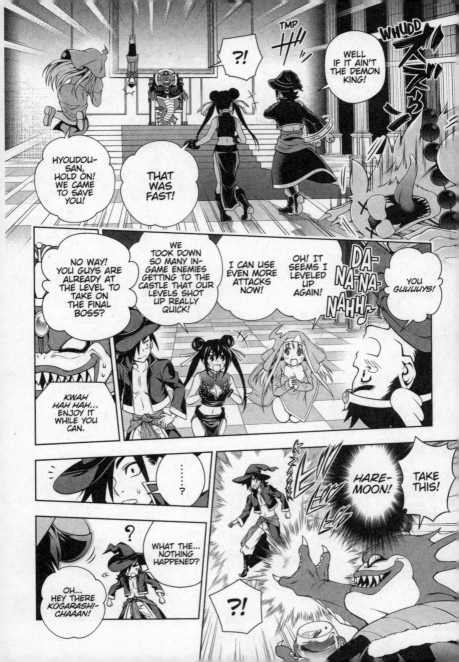

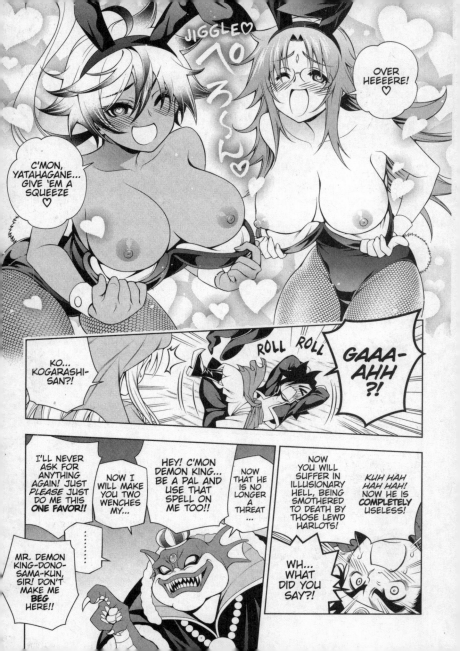

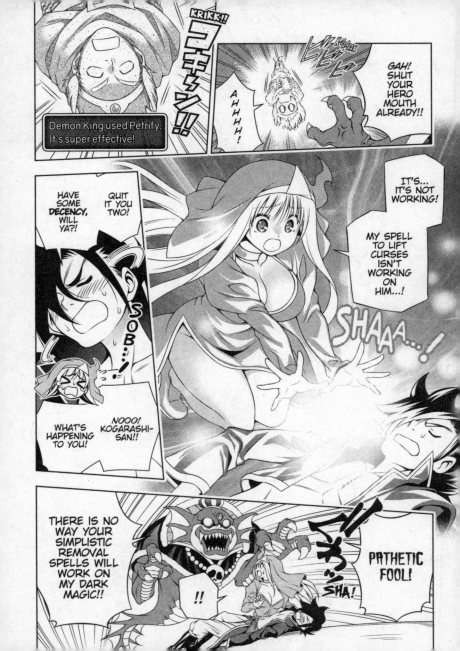

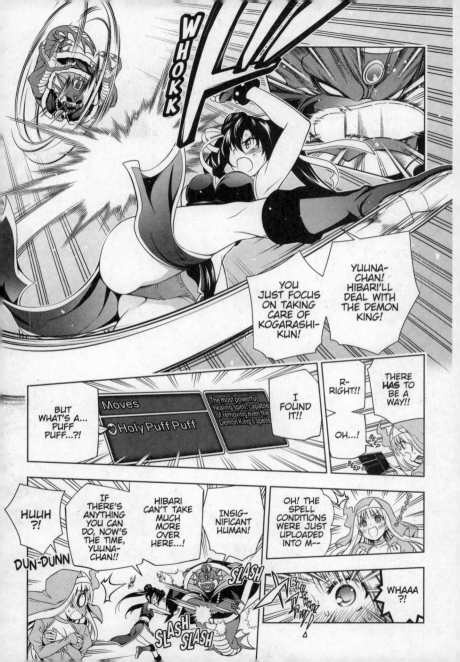

WHOKK

YOU JUST FOCUS ON TAKING CARE OF KOGARASHI-KUN!

YUUNA-CHAN! HIBARI'LL DEAL WITH THE DEMON KING!

BUT WHAT'S A... PUFF PUFF...?!

Moves

Holy Puff Puff

The most powerful healing spell, capable of removing even the Demon King's spells.

I FOUND IT!!

R-RIGHT!!

OH...!

THERE HAS TO BE A WAY!!

BEEP

BEEP

HUUH ?!

IF THERE'S ANYTHING YOU CAN DO, NOW'S THE TIME, YUUNA-CHAN!!

HIBARI CAN'T TAKE MUCH MORE OVER HERE...!

INSIGNIFICANT HUMAN!

OH! THE SPELL CONDITIONS WERE JUST UPLOADED INTO M--

WHAAA ?!

DUN-DUNN

SLASH

SLASH SLASH

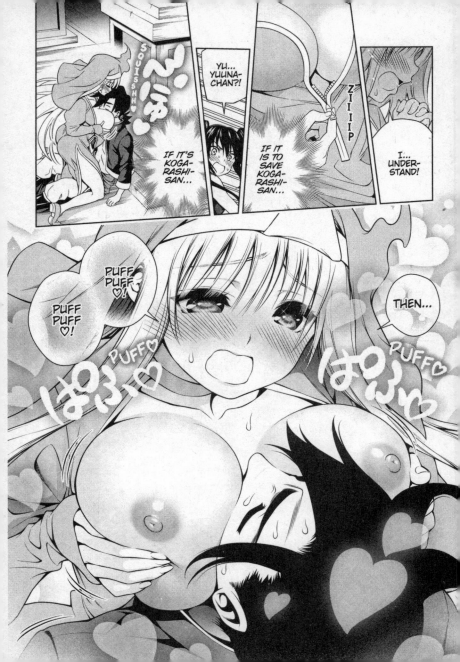

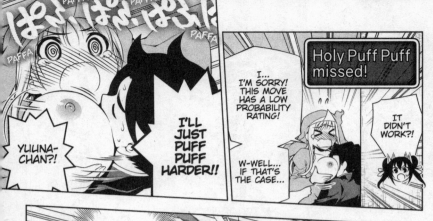

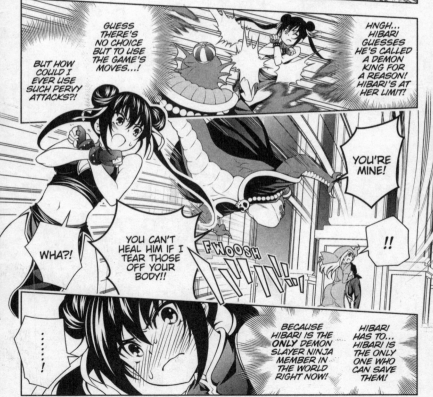

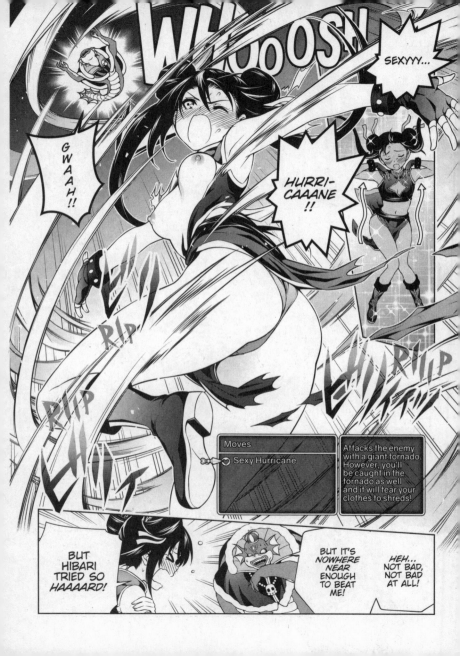

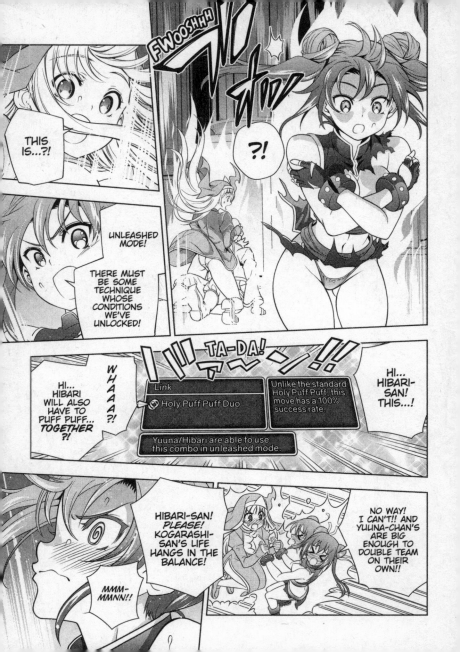

FWOOSHHH

?!

THIS IS...?!

UNLEASHED MODE!

THERE MUST BE SOME TECHNIQUE WHOSE CONDITIONS WE'VE UNLOCKED!

TA-DA!

WHAAAA?!

HI... HIBARI WILL ALSO HAVE TO PUFF PUFF... *TOGETHER* ?!

HI... HIBARI-SAN! THIS...!

Link

◉ Holy Puff Puff Duo

Unlike the standard Holy Puff Puff, this move has a 100% success rate.

Yuuna/Hibari are able to use this combo in unleashed mode.

HIBARI-SAN! PLEASE! KOGARASHI-SAN'S LIFE HANGS IN THE BALANCE!

MMM-MMNN!!

NO WAY! I CAN'T!! AND YUUNA-CHAN'S ARE BIG ENOUGH TO DOUBLE TEAM ON THEIR OWN!!

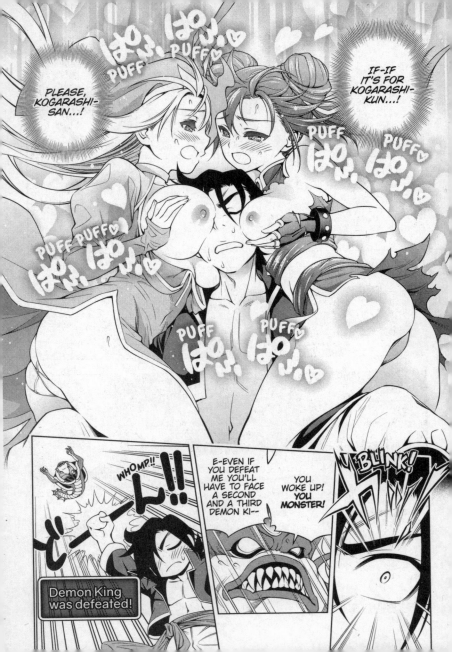

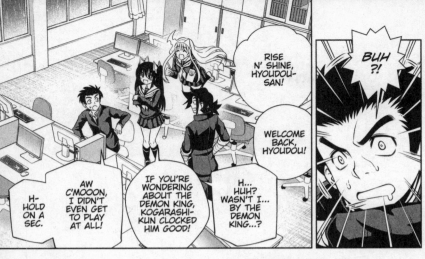

RISE N' SHINE, HYOUDOU-SAN!

WELCOME BACK, HYOUDOU!

BUH ?!

H-HOLD ON A SEC.

AW C'MOOON, I DIDN'T EVEN GET TO PLAY AT ALL!

IF YOU'RE WONDERING ABOUT THE DEMON KING, KOGARASHI-KUN CLOCKED HIM GOOD!

H... HUH? WASN'T I... BY THE DEMON KING...?

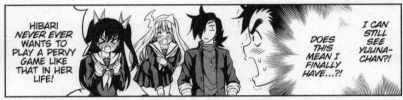

HIBARI NEVER EVER WANTS TO PLAY A PERVY GAME LIKE THAT IN HER LIFE!

DOES THIS MEAN I FINALLY HAVE...?!

I CAN STILL SEE YUUNA-CHAN?!

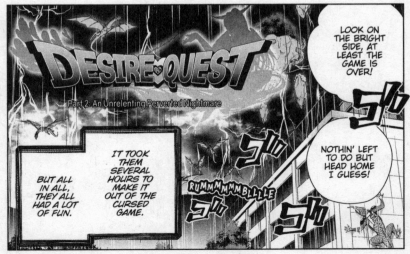

DESIRE♥QUEST

Part 2: An Unrelenting Perverted Nightmare

LOOK ON THE BRIGHT SIDE, AT LEAST THE GAME IS OVER!

NOTHIN' LEFT TO DO BUT HEAD HOME I GUESS!

BUT ALL IN ALL, THEY ALL HAD A LOT OF FUN.

IT TOOK THEM SEVERAL HOURS TO MAKE IT OUT OF THE CURSED GAME.

RUMMMMMMBLLLE

9 White Day Fantasy (End)

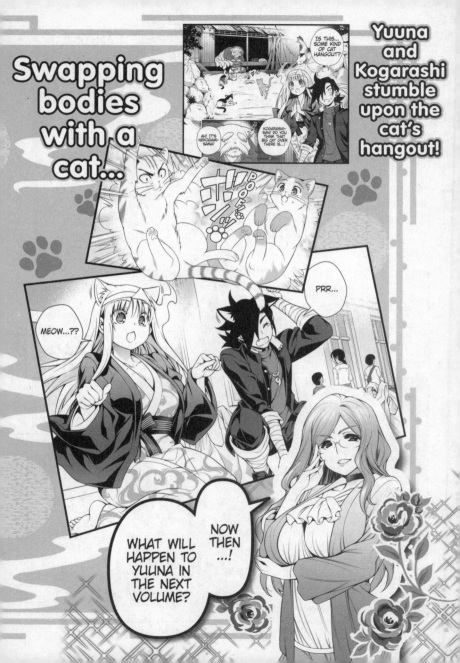

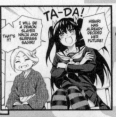

Parent Teacher Conferences!!

So close, yet so far.

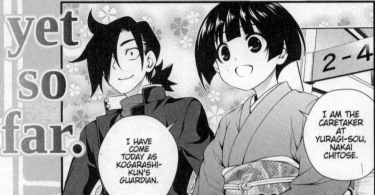

I HAVE COME TODAY AS KOGARASHI-KUN'S GUARDIAN.

I AM THE CARETAKER AT YURAGI-SOU, NAKAI CHITOSE.

2 - 4

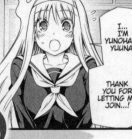

I... I'M YUNOHANA YUUNA!

THANK YOU FOR LETTING ME JOIN...!

Yuuna and the Haunted Hot Springs

The super popular manga series...

Kogarashi and Yuuna's feelings—mutual, yet un-noticed...

Volume 10 is coming soon!

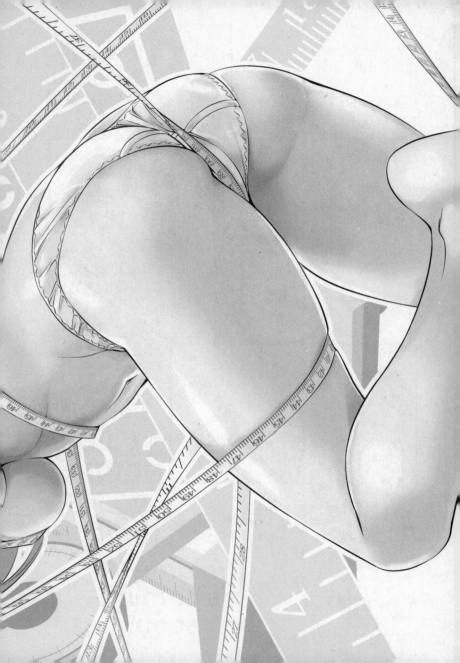

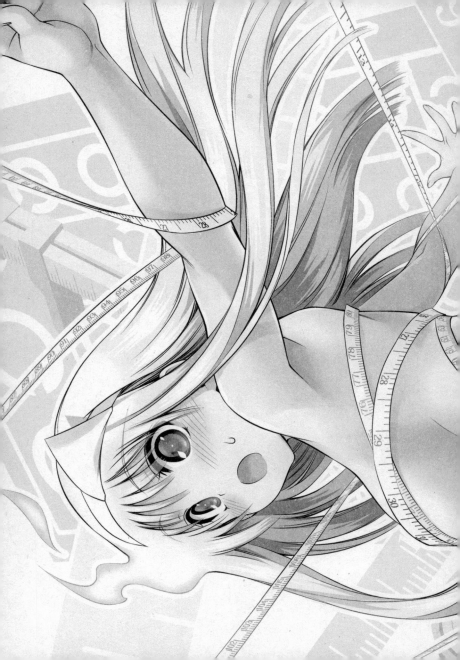

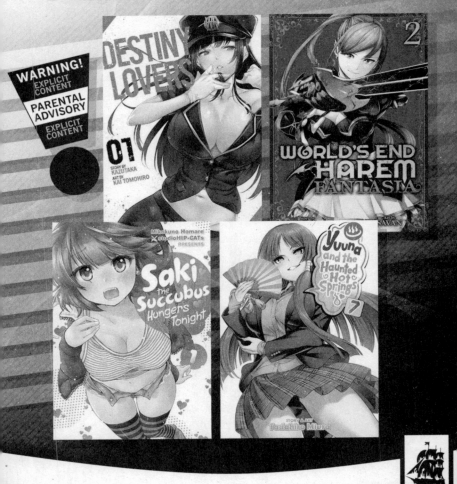

SEVEN SEAS' GHOST SHIP PRESENTS

Yuuna and the Haunted Hot Springs VOL.9

story and art by TADAHIRO MIURA

TRANSLATION
Thomas Zimmerman

ADAPTATION
David Lumsdon

LETTERING AND RETOUCH
Phil Christie

LOGO DESIGN
KC Fabellon

COVER DESIGN
Nicky Lim

PROOFREADER
Kurestin Armada

EDITOR
Casey Lucas

PREPRESS TECHNICIAN
Rhiannon Rasmussen-Silverstein

MANAGING EDITOR
Julie Davis

ASSOCIATE PUBLISHER
Adam Arnold

PUBLISHER
Jason DeAngelis

Seven Seas press and purchase enquiries can be sent to Marketing Manager
Lianne Sentar at press@gomanga.com. Information regarding the distribution
and purchase of digital editions is available from Digital Manager CK Russell
at digital@gomanga.com.

Seven Seas, Ghost Ship, and their accompanying logos are trademarks of
Seven Seas Entertainment. All rights reserved.

ISBN: 978-1-947804-53-1

Printed in Canada

First Printing: May 2020

10 9 8 7 6 5 4 3 2 1

FOLLOW US ONLINE: *www.ghostshipmanga.com*

READING DIRECTIONS

This book reads from *right to left*, Japanese style.
If this is your first time reading manga, you start
reading from the top right panel on each page and
take it from there. If you get lost, just follow the
numbered diagram here. It may seem backwards at
first, but you'll get the hang of it! Have fun!!

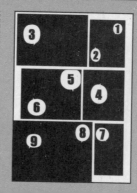